S0-AAE-948

Unspeakable!

A Mother's Journey

Colleen,

Thank you for
making this book extra
special!

Kay Armstrong Baker

Kay Armstrong Baker

outskirtspress

DENVER, COLORADO

The opinions expressed in this manuscript are solely the opinions of the author and do not represent the opinions or thoughts of the publisher. The author has represented and warranted full ownership and/or legal right to publish all the materials in this book.

Unspeakable!
A Mother's Journey
All Rights Reserved.
Copyright © 2014 Kay Armstrong Baker
v5.0 r1.0

Cover Image by Kay Armstrong Baker

This book may not be reproduced, transmitted, or stored in whole or in part by any means, including graphic, electronic, or mechanical without the express written consent of the publisher except in the case of brief quotations embodied in critical articles and reviews.

Outskirts Press, Inc.
http://www.outskirtspress.com

ISBN: 978-1-4787-1081-3

Outskirts Press and the "OP" logo are trademarks belonging to Outskirts Press, Inc.

PRINTED IN THE UNITED STATES OF AMERICA

Dedicated to parents who live with this loss

Acknowledgments

Tom Benjamin
Betty Caldwell
Barry Frieman
Martha Fulda
Rev. Paige Getty
Helen Heffer
Carolyn Johnson
Margaret Lumphrey
Jan McCormick
Marie Sawyer
Joanne Settel
Gene Somers
Trish Steinhilber

Table of Contents

Introduction

I began writing after the death of my daughter, Courtney, on August 27, 2000. When I began writing, it was a way to express my emotions in written form. It soon became a vital and essential outlet for me. I never intended for my personal account to be published until several friends, as well as parents who had lost children, encouraged me to do so. I have included stories and pictures of Courtney to provide the reader with a glimpse into the life of the daughter we lost.

At the time of Courtney's death, I was a realtor. Work, as well as travel, retreats, music, time with family and special events, were a vital diversion. Grief sapped my energy. I had meditated, exercised, and practiced yoga for many years. All of these activities grounded me, released endorphins, and helped me get to work. I can't emphasize this enough.

I also shared the many instances of "magical thinking." This was not just the first year after Courtney's death, but it continues, at times, to this day. Some days I still find it extremely difficult to accept the reality of her death. The death of a child ,no matter their age, is such a nightmare that I doubt many parents truly believe it happened! My child has to exist somewhere; her essence has to be alive!

It doesn't matter why or how our children died. Their deaths leave a

UNSPEAKABLE!

tremendous void that settles within the very core of our being. My intension is to share my personal experiences in the hope that you will identify with, gain comfort from and know you are not alone on this convoluted journey called grief.

My memoir is also for family and friends as well as professionals who support us as we stumble along this path of the "unspeakable."

CHAPTER 1

Shock and Disbelief

August 30, 2000

On August 27, between three and four o'clock in the afternoon, the unthinkable happened. Our daughter, Courtney, died! As I write these words, it seems preposterous, yet at the same time, her death was what we feared either consciously or subconsciously for 28½ years.

The month of August was one thing after another: dehydration, migraines, or both—plus multiple trips to the emergency room for arrhythmia. On August 11, she was dehydrated. On the Wednesday prior to her death—unbeknownst to us at the time—she spent eleven hours in the ER with a migraine that finally stopped after 250 milligrams of Demerol. She hadn't called us because she said there was nothing we could have done. Sometime during that month, she told me that she was getting tired of the nausea from the pregnancy and the headaches. She hoped the headaches would stop now that she had passed her third month, but it seemed like everything was getting worse.

Courtney planned to have dinner with us that Sunday. Brian, her husband, had just left for Fort Benning, Georgia to begin officer candidate school. That afternoon Courtney left a message that she was getting yet another "killer" migraine and was going back to her apartment.

Her roommate, Jane, told us Courtney came home and sat down on the couch after taking her medication. She began complaining of blurred vision and numbness in her arm, and then suddenly, she stiffened and fell off the couch. Jane administered CPR and called 911. The ambulance arrived within five minutes, but to Jane, it seemed like forever. The EMT's tried to resuscitate Courtney but there was no response. According to the nurse at the hospital, they administered CPR again and could not get her heart to respond.

John was home. I was negotiating two offers involving the sale of a condo. I finished between four and four thirty and called him to see if he needed me to stop and get anything for dinner. That is when John told me that Courtney's roommate had just called. She'd informed him that Courtney had had a bad reaction to her medication and was taken to the ER in Randallstown. He told me to come home, and we'd drive to the hospital together.

Another visit to the ER! Although I was concerned, I knew I'd feel better once I saw and talked to her. Courtney always landed on her feet.

We arrived at the ER. I told the receptionist who we were. A security guard led us to a "family room." I knew that this was not the usual procedure, and I was beginning to worry that Courtney had lost the baby. Her roommate and two or three other ambulance friends, whom I recognized as Courtney's co-workers from the Life Star ambulance company where she worked as an EMT, were there. Jane was crying. There was also a policeman which I thought was unusual. He asked us if we were Courtney's parents. We told him we were. He then excused himself to go and get the doctor.

John and I will never forget the next scene. The doctor came in. She sat down and said, "Courtney has died." Just like that. "Courtney has died."

We have replayed that scene over and over again in our minds. It felt like an electric shock had coursed through my body! We felt disbelief and dismay. What we had feared for so long had finally happened.

John began pacing, his hand on his chest, saying over and over "It hurts! Oh, how it hurts." My body was the first to respond to the shock. I told the nurse I had to use the bathroom. When I got back, I went to see Courtney. They had "cleaned her up," but she still had a tube in her mouth. It was so surreal. She was so still. I felt a soft touch on my elbow. I turned but there was no one there. Courtney was beginning to turn cold, although her color was still normal.

John could not bring himself to see her and never did. I stayed with her a bit, but then felt I needed to be with John. There was nothing more I could do for her. I kept returning to the room where she lay, as if she would suddenly awake and need to see us. What a horrible feeling. After all the years of Courtney coming through everything that had been thrown at her, it was over.

The next thing we had to do was contact her husband, Brian, in Georgia. It took awhile to locate him, as he was training in the woods somewhere. After an hour or so—we lost track of time—he called the room where families stay during a crisis. His worst fears had been realized. He told us that he would make arrangements to come as soon as he could.

We left the hospital in the middle of a terrible thunderstorm. We could hardly see. The defroster was barely working. The wind buffeted the car, and it was hard for John to keep it steady. How we got home that night, I'll never know!

We began calling our close friends and family to tell them the awful news. We didn't know where Courtney's brother, Jason, was; he had just picked up his girlfriend in San Francisco and was heading up the coast. He called the next night from San Jose. Our friends there had to tell him the bad news.

The last few days have been a blur. We can't sleep. I can't eat. The pain and horror reflected on the faces of our friends is palpable. People want to do something but of course there is nothing they can do. Food is pouring in. Our family and friends arrived on Monday, and we met with our minister to begin planning the memorial service.

(The following eulogies I want to include from the point of view of others.)

Eulogy
August 30, 2000
Rev. Cindy Snavely

As her family told me about Courtney, I was reminded of a song from The Sound of Music. *It is the one that goes, "She is gentle. She is wild. She's a riddle. She's a child. She's a headache. She's an angel. She's a girl." Courtney's mother said, "She had a very strong will. Courtney blew things out of proportion." Her father said, "She was stubborn." Her husband, Brian, said, "She was passionate about everything."*

"How do you solve a problem like Courtney? How do you catch a

cloud and pin it down? How do you keep a wave upon the sand? How do you hold a moonbeam in your hand?" Her mother recalls seeing Courtney as a newborn in the incubator. The set of her jaw told her that this baby was going to survive. Courtney grew into a sensitive and determined young woman, one of the most giving of people.

Strays tugged at Courtney's heart strings. Animals were always going to stay just until another home could be found. But sometimes there was no other home. Courtney has left Brian with three cats. For a while they had four. There was the pet boa constrictor that was sick and died. For a while there was talk of a ferret, but no ferret ever became part of the household.

It was not her giving heart but her heart condition that meant that Courtney had to deal with things that most of her peers did not. Her mother said that she seemed as though she was a 28-year-old living in a 78-year-old body toward the end. All her life she tried hard to be normal and fit in. She wanted to be like everyone else, have what others had—a husband, a child, a family. Because she wasn't like everyone else, her point of view on much of life had a different slant. She saw life in unique ways.

Courtney loved Jim Henson's Muppets and Shel Silverstein's poetry. Courtney felt something of her childhood died when Henson died. If some part of us continues after death, perhaps Courtney is with Henson and Silverstein now creating a drama to be acted by Muppets. She, too, wrote poetry in high school and as a young adult.

Courtney loved theater, movies, soap operas, and TV shows. In high school she had an entire script of The Breakfast Club *memorized. Movies featuring Molly Ringwald and other actors and actresses of the "Brat Pack" were favorites. She would watch the same movies and the same episodes of shows over and over. She knew most of the lines in the episodes of Roseanne.*

Because of her heart condition, Courtney spent a lot of time recently in emergency rooms. Her mother kidded Courtney that she liked going to the emergency room because it was another chance to observe dramas. Stuck in a curtained emergency room, Courtney would listen to the stories of the patients and their families on her right and on her left and across the way.

I suspect that Courtney did not really like the emergency rooms, but she did like cemeteries. In a way they, too, were dramas, bits of stories written in epitaphs—the dates of births and deaths and who was buried next to whom. She enjoyed wandering among the stones. Now Courtney, too, is gone. In some ways the drama of her life is over, but in others it is not. Who she was and what she did has influenced who we are. Within our lives, Courtney's story continues on.

Eulogy
August 30, 2000
Brian Slosman, Courtney's Husband

It took me a long time to think of something that I wanted to say about Courtney. I spent a lot of time confused because I did not know whom I was supposed to say it to. Was I supposed to address our family and friends, merely to share my thoughts, or was I supposed to pretend that this was a last chance to talk to Courtney herself? Was I supposed to share a memory that I hold dear, a funny story that was uniquely Courtney, an excerpt from a children's story, or a bit of poetry with some meaning? Was I supposed to remember Courtney when she was alive and what she meant to me?

My problem is not that I don't have anything to say but that I have too much to say. My memory of Courtney and my relationship with her was unique—at least as unique as the people involved. I know her as her husband, a relationship severed by death. However, Courtney was also my best friend and my companion. Words cannot describe my loss, or even what I had with Courtney before that loss. Courtney was a gift, and I was blessed to be able to spend her final years with her—three years as her husband. What I gained in our relationship makes all of this bearable.

I feel for those who find it difficult to share my positive outlook. I feel for those whose own identity has been changed by her passing. It is much different for me as Courtney's husband from John, Courtney's father; Kay, Courtney's mother; and Jason, Courtney's brother. For John and Kay and Jason, my heart breaks for you more than for myself, and I wish you anything that allows you the strength to redefine yourself in a way to continue but also to remember. When I wrote you that poem, "Bound in Marriage, United in Grief, Family Forever," I meant it. I look forward to the sharing of more joyous occasions.

Courtney had more family and many friends, of which the closest are now present. For you, Debbie, Jennifer, and Rick, I look forward to the day when we are able to celebrate Courtney and who she was without the overwhelming grief that we now feel.

To my family, I know you shared in the tragedy of Courtney's passing, especially in the depth of my loss. Through me, you have also lost a daughter or a sister. I look forward to the time when we can share my happiness rather than my sadness.

To Courtney, I hope that in your passing and in whatever way you may have remained cognizant, you know how much I love you. You were so precious and dear to me; you were my celebration of life. I

7

wish I could have shared with you what would have been an over-abundance of joy with the birth of our son who has accompanied you in death. Even now I enjoy knowing how much joy the beating of his own heart meant to you and how I was a part of that. Without words, and him without a name, I have also grieved his passing with his mother. Today, feeling as afflicted as I do, I still would not have changed a thing or wished anything different about the time we had together. This is hard right now but not nearly as hard as imagining my life without you. I know you loved me, too.

One of your favorite poems gives me comfort:

> *Merry meet and Merry part*

> *Bright the Cheeks*

> *Warm the Heart*

> *Merry meet and Merry part*

> *And merry meet again.*

September 6, 2000

I just remembered that a couple of weeks before Courtney died, we were sitting in the family room. I was trying to pin her down as to whether she was going to stay at the house and take care of Garfield (our cat), or whether I would have to make other arrangements while we were in France. She had avoided giving me an answer, so I kept pressing her. I also asked her if she was afraid of something happening to her dad and me. Brian had told us that Courtney had a fear of us dying. I can't remember what she said, but I remember what I said. I told her that "naturally" we would die before her, just as her grandparents had gone before us.

I asked her if she was afraid of staying by herself. Courtney had always rather matter-of-factly said there were ghosts in the house, specifically a lady and a little boy. I asked her whether she was un-comfortable about that. She said no. In fact, "The Lady" had moved over to her apartment! Whatever premonitions she was having, she would not say.

Séances

Courtney always was fascinated by the "other side," i.e., witches, ghosts, and spirits. The following memory stands out in my mind, as it was so typical of her in grade school. I also want to point out that this, as well as similar experiences, always took place when her analytical father was out of town!

One day after school, Courtney came home and told me they were having séances at school. She was very enthusiastic about it. By this time in my parenting career, I had learned to just say, "Oh?" when Courtney was telling me something like this. In a few days, she came home and told me they could no longer have séances at school. Again my response was the same in the hope that she would elaborate. Instead Courtney went on with her after-school activities and said nothing more about it!

I had a hunch that it must have been Courtney's idea and persuaded other girls to join her. Eventually, the teachers found out what was going on and put a stop to it. That was Courtney being Courtney.

UNSPEAKABLE!

That weekend Courtney and two other neighborhood girls came running into the house, all talking at once. They were obviously frightened. Courtney said that they had seen "Bloody Mary"! Apparently, they had been conducting a séance with a Ouija board in the garage of one of the other girls. It was dark and more conducive for a séance, I guess. All three said they saw an image they called "Bloody Mary." Naturally, it scared the wits out of them! Courtney cut her foot in the race to open the garage door, and it was bleeding. That fueled their imagination even further. Courtney claimed that it was Bloody Mary who had done it.

I sat the little girls down and gave them some cookies and juice. I told them I could see that something had truly scared them. I went on to say that I didn't know or couldn't judge what had happened, but that it would be a good idea to leave activities such as this alone. That seemed to help calm them down, and they went off to play something else as if nothing had happened.

Around midnight, after we had gone to bed, Courtney woke up screaming. I ran to her room, jarred from a deep sleep. She said she saw Bloody Mary again. The dream had definitely scared her. All that drama kept us up for hours. Courtney and her brother, Jason, ended up in my bed for the rest of the night.

To this day, I don't know what she saw or heard. Nor can I shine any light on it from an analytical point of view. It was most likely a bad dream following on the heels of the incident in Christi's garage. I was Courtney's mother, not a psychologist or a paranormal practitioner. I made it a point throughout her life to be open and not deride her for her perceptions. All I can tell you is that she always saw life from a different perspective.

September 6, 2000

(I kept a diary during our trip to France. We felt we needed to get away and followed through with our plans. It turned out to be the best decision we'd ever made!)

Paris is everything people have said, painted, sang or written about it! "How ya gonna keep 'em down on the farm after they've seen Paree?"

We got settled in the Ascot Opera Hotel. After a shower we took the metro to Père Lachaise, the cemetery where Chopin, Bizet, and Jim Morrison are buried. It seemed strange to be going to a cemetery after Courtney's death! However, it did serve two purposes: it reinforced that Courtney had died, and it lifted my spirits to pay my respects to Chopin.

We did a lot of sightseeing, eating, and a lot of walking. Amid all of this, I was thinking about Courtney. She would have loved to see the gargoyles at Notre Dame and the medieval museum. How can we be having such an experience and at the same time grieving for our daughter?

September 7, 2000

Just a month ago, I accompanied Courtney to her OB appointment and heard the baby's heart beat. Now, a month later, I'm reeling from her death.

UNSPEAKABLE!

Notre Dame is magnificent! Beautiful stained glass! Even though it had a lot of people in it, there was a good feeling about it. Peaceful. We lit a candle for Courtney at the shrine of Joan of Arc.

September 10, 2000

We are on a six-passenger houseboat. Sunflowers are everywhere. Acres and acres of them! Every flower shop has beautiful bouquets of sunflowers. Courtney, our "Kansas Sunflower," is never far away.

September 16, 2000

All along our cruise, people have been friendly and patient with us. Periodically the horror of Courtney's death resurfaces and then recedes. We've had trouble sleeping. The entire trip has been a good escape for us. We'll have the rest of our lives to cope with the reality of Courtney's death.

September 30, 2000

One month later and home from France, I cycle between resignation and tears of disbelief. How could this happen? I go back through the last year or two. John says, "It won't change anything, so why put yourself through it?" Work will help if it will only pick up. At least we have our minds on something else for a time. Jason is at Kripalu, an ashram in Massachusetts, for a three-month "work/study" program. He thinks about Courtney, but

Kripalu is so removed from everything I think it helps him. Going back home will not be easy, as it was not easy for John and me.

We go out to dinner with friends, go for walks, shop, etc., as if we are zombies. We're numb yet we're raw like an open wound. When I feel resigned and there are no more tears to shed, I feel as though I am enclosed in a box. At the same time, I feel exposed and bleeding. What a life! What is the point? Is there a point? If Courtney does exist, what is she feeling? Does she miss us? Is she as upset as we are, or is it, as some people believe, a sense of sublime peace?

A longtime friend called the other night and said she had gotten great comfort from a discussion of reincarnation at her church. I believe in reincarnation, but it does me no good at this time. We're adjusting to Courtney not being with us *physically*. No amount of theorizing about the afterlife does much good when we're waiting for a phone call or for her to come through the door.

October 7, 2000

I've slept well this week even though I'm alone. John is in Brussels; Jason is due back from Kripalu tomorrow. Thursday was a bad day and yet a good one. I went to the clothing sale at Johns Hopkins Hospital with some friends. It was fun trying on all those neat clothes. Then, suddenly, I became tired and bored. I remembered that Courtney and I had gone last year. I asked some of the volunteers where the proceeds went from the sales. They told me some of the money raised bought beds for parents whose children were on the pediatric ward. Under normal circumstances, I would have shared my experience on a pediatric ward 27½ years ago but could not do it now. Instead I went into the bathroom and started crying. The longer I was gone from home, the more I felt the grief welling up in me.

UNSPEAKABLE!

We had a nice lunch, but overall I was distracted. It seems as though I have to watch my time out among "normal" people. If it becomes too long, I start feeling the urgency to return home.

I'm starting to evaluate my relationship with Courtney. I shouldn't go there because it makes no difference anyway. I felt sometimes as though she and I were very much like my mother-in-law and me: "two ships passing in the night." I have to believe our relationship was better than that. Courtney and I enjoyed theater, music, movies, the supernatural, etc. Outside of those activities, it was hard to find things to talk about. Her health was an ever-present specter the last two years, which was not openly discussed but covered over with a monologue about movies, a crisis at work, and soap operas—anything but what was really going on. It was too scary. I said I wouldn't go there, and yet I have.

A strange thing happened this morning. A friend had given me a card that she had made. It had a photo she had taken of a blue heron. At about seven o'clock, as I was lying in bed, trying to get up, the picture peeled off the card and fell to the floor, leaving the card on the bureau. Pat had looked up in *Animal Speaks*, by Ted Andrews, what the heron signified. *(We had seen herons everywhere along the canal in France.)* It described Courtney: unusual, jack-of-all-trades; no structure, no stability or security; untraditional. At any rate, I spoke out loud and told "Courtney" if that was a sign, she needed to do something else that couldn't be explained away.

John is having a rough time of it. He told me last week that he'd had another lucid dream. I strongly feel that this is some kind of communication from Courtney. He says they are just dreams. He'll tell me about this latest one when he gets home. John has always had special dreams; he sometimes knows things before they happen; such as his best friend dying in Vietnam, his father's heart attacks, and his brother's near-death experience after a car accident. Jason's dreams have Courtney in them, but she is simply present.

October 11, 2000

I dreamed I saw Courtney in the hall. I said, "Courtney!" and grabbed her hand. She continued to walk up the stairs. She was in a plain white shift with a necklace, and her hair was pulled back. No glasses. She just kept moving past me and through my grasp but did turn to look back at me as she ascended the stairs. The stairwell was full of light. I went into our bedroom and was talking to a younger John, Jason, and Courtney. I told them what I had seen. It was as if I were talking about "The Lady." When I said she seemed distant and angry, the younger Courtney agreed. I woke up! Maybe it wasn't anger but only she had to go and I couldn't hold on to her.

November 5, 2000

I've had so many fleeting thoughts and feelings this past month. Today I'm going to try to remember as much as I can.

One morning I was thinking of Glenda, Courtney's pediatric cardiology nurse. It came to me that Courtney was like Dorothy in *The Wizard of Oz,* who found herself in a strange land. The doctors were the wizard, the witches were her protectors as well as those who challenged her, and her friends were with her all along the way home. It came to me that she has gone home.

I keep looking for a sign from Courtney, but if she is sending any, we aren't picking them up because we're expecting them to be and look like something else. Nothing at Halloween or November 1. I don't know what I expect. Courtney and I would joke that when John or I died, we would try hard to send a message from "beyond" to signal that we existed. We even laughed that if I died first, I would have to conjure up something spectacular to prove to John that I existed in some other form. When Courtney and I would have this conversation, I never consciously thought that she would die first.

As the days go by, now ten weeks today, what we are feeling—at least what I'm feeling is the "dead" silence. No phone ringing; no door opening and slamming, definitely making her presence known; no lively chatter. Years ago, my mother described her feelings about her brother's death as "He's just away." Was this denial or simply my mother's Midwestern stoicism and her way of coping?

I need to write down, wherever I am, when insights come to me because I forget them as quickly as they appear. I know I have a lot to write about, but it is not in my consciousness now.

We finally got the autopsy report. Jason had to drive into Baltimore to get it. The cause of death was checked "unknown." Somehow the medication plus the rapid heartbeat she'd had contributed to her death. The fetus, a boy, seventy-two grams, was perfect. Oh, the pain! It's unbearable!

John, Jason, and I had a good conversation about Courtney. We all felt that she knew her days were numbered, but she only indirectly communicated that to us. Now that we finally have the report, will it bring a little more closure? Possibly, but our journey is far from over. We will never be the same. Everything will be remembered as happening before Courtney died or after Courtney died. John goes to work every day, and life goes on until he gets home. Surprisingly,

I've had some business. Finding new business takes so much energy. I need to be busy, but at the same time I want to hide.

Again I'm sitting here knowing there are things, memories, and insights to be put to paper, and yet I'm blank.

November 11, 2000

I talked to Brian today after he received the autopsy report. He was very upset. He feels that if he had been with her, she wouldn't have died. He's naturally upset about the baby. What words can clearly describe our pain?

I'm exhausted. I had to keep it together while showing property. Maybe that was best rather than at home screaming and tearing my clothes.

(I've used rune stones from time to time. I draw a stone randomly and meditate on the message of that particular stone.) The stone I drew today was about a spiritual birth and that fear would be a part of it. It went on to say that I would be in a crisis, have a difficult time. Everything is a test.

November 12, 2000

We've spent two days on the Eastern Shore with friends. We went to the Waterfowl Festival and had a "good" time. It was a pleasant diversion. I almost bought a painting or a photograph of a blue heron, but nothing grabbed both of us. I dreamed last night of a lamb being washed down a stream over a small falls. It was alive. The dream changed to a child in a lamb-like "cuddle suit." The dream changed again. I had gotten mad at a friend or snapped at her or something. I had to apologize, but she kept saying that I might need to have treatment if I didn't get better.

I awoke and thought about the dreams and the meaning of the lamb: Jesus looking for the lost lamb; Courtney's baby; me, am I lost? I went back to sleep with the song, "Someone to Watch Over Me" in my head and thinking about my spiritual guides.

Sundays are always difficult. It's been eleven weeks since Courtney died. I dropped John off at the airport after irritating him with my incessant questions about his feelings. I guess what really set him off was my observation that he doesn't look or act any different when we are out with other people. He took that as if I were saying he wasn't grieving as much as me. So now we'll get a breather from each other. Hopefully, John's friend Vincent is in Los Alamos, so he'll have someone to talk to.

Tonight, I heard Forrest Church speak to a group at our Church. He is the minister at the New York City Unitarian Universalist church and son of the late Senator Frank Church. He has written several books but preferred to talk about the election and that we all need to keep to the high road. He emphasized that only in relationships can we truly find ourselves. By putting others down for their beliefs, we put ourselves down also. Energy expended on hating or being angry with someone does you no good. Forgiveness is liberating. At any rate, I came away with some insight. I need to be caring for myself by not worrying about business, etc. I began to re-read the book *How to Stop Worrying and Start Living* by Dale Carnegie.

November 13, 2000

(At times in an attempt to cope with my grief, I found that listing the positive events or accomplishments during the day was helpful.)

This has been a good day. Why?

- The weekend away.

- A card from old friends.

- I spent the rest of Sunday in silence except to answer the phone.

- I made a number of cold calls.

- I read some of *Stop Worrying*.

- I shared our trip to France with the sailing club.

November 14, 2000

I dreamed that I was holding Courtney as a baby or maybe looking at pictures of the two of us. A message or thought that I remember was "All part of one" or "You were one or are one." In other dreams last night she was just there.

November 15, 2000

I'm finding that if I dress for work and have a list of calls to make, I do better for that period of time.

November 20, 2000

I'm at a new stage. The shock has worn off. I'm mad as hell and depressed. It takes twice the energy to do anything, let alone try to work. I simply want to be alone, and at the same time, I know that it is not good for long periods of time.

I'm angry at Courtney for leaving us, and now we're left "holding the bag," facing the holidays and life without her—nothing to look forward to. The cold, hard reality has hit. She is gone. It is permanent. We're left to pick up the pieces. A close friend of Courtney's feels guilty for not hanging out with her that day. Then reason takes over. Courtney must have been in a lot of pain. Get help! Then the metaphysical takes over: nothing happens by accident. (The card from *The Power Deck*, by Lynn V. Andrews, and card paintings by Rob Schouten—"Time" was the card I pulled the morning before she died.) *"What is time that it has such power to change all that exists back into dust? What is this unseen force like the wind that can shape the land and our lives?"*

I'm confused, angry, tired, depressed, and I don't know what to do except bear it.

November 23, 2000

After two days of crying off and on, the second of the holidays is here. I went into Baltimore and volunteered at Bea Grady's Thanksgiving dinner for the poor from nine to noon. That was a good thing to do and pretty much kept my mind off Courtney. Did not—could not—discuss why I was there volunteering.

I need to list what I have to be thankful for to get me through the rest of the day:

- I was Courtney's mother for 28½ years, through thick and thin.

- Jason—I couldn't ask for a better son.

- Having John as my husband for thirty-five years—his patience, his humor, just him.

- Brian, my son-in-law. What a good choice Courtney made!

- My career in real estate.

- My friends—the ones I've made recently as well as those I've had for over forty years.

- My cousins, my remaining aunts.

- My music ability.

- The many countries I've visited.

- My excellent health, which I've had all my life.

There may be more, but this has helped to make me feel that I'm not alone and my life is not over—at least for now!

December 5, 2000

The pall lifted for a short time after Thanksgiving weekend. It was difficult seeing Brian for the first time since Courtney died. We had Rick, Jen, Debbie, and Brian for spaghetti. I was totally exhausted afterward. John developed a cold the next day. The pall lifted for me, I guess, because I was busy chasing my tail in real estate!

UNSPEAKABLE!

The pall returned with the sound of Christmas music and people talking excitedly about parties, plans, gifts, etc. I feel as though I've got a disease, a wound. It must be visible by the way people I know look at me. I've started to wear my contacts part of the day. I feel exposed, naked without the glasses. My eyes, I fear, tell it all: the pain, strain, and stress. With the glasses, I feel I can hide the horror at least a little.

I thought I had stopped this day's ramblings. I picked up the book, *Grieving the Loss of Someone You Love,* by Raymond R. Mitsch and Lynn Brookside. I opened it to the chapter entitled "Feeling Like a Leper". That's exactly how I feel at times! It's interesting all the co-incidences, prophecies, and premonitions that surround Courtney's life and death.

December 7, 2000

Fourteen years ago today, my father died. It feels a lot longer!

This "grief process" is so interesting. (That's an understatement!) "Grief" releases its hold on you, and you think you have "moved on" until you're yanked back into its iron grasp once again.

I went into the office this afternoon. A note from a good friend told me that the agents in the office would light a candle for Courtney on Sunday night at seven. It is a support group for parents who have lost children. This friend has done so much for me. I don't know how I'll ever repay her.

December 14, 2000

Brian graduated today from OCS in Georgia. It was his day, and we all rose to the occasion. We took lots of pictures. We gave him three books on Buddhism. Wherever we were, Courtney was there. Breakfast: an empty chair. The graduation: an empty chair. Lunch: an empty chair. Jason noticed it, too.

Brian's apartment is very nice. I think of the things she's missing: formals, the apartment, and the new challenges as an officer's wife. During dinner: no empty chair but an empty table next to us. One of Courtney's friends mentioned the game, "Name that Tune." Courtney would play it with the guys in the ambulance while she and Jen were dispatching on the night shift. What an imp!

Courtney was always two steps ahead of us—probably more. It's amazing to me that her "creativity" continued after she left home and spilled over into the workplace. No wonder she had so many jobs! She always seemed to me to be a square peg trying to fit into a round hole.

(It's difficult for a grieving parent to avoid feelings of guilt-thoughts such as "I should have" or "I wasn't a good parent". It's important not to remain in these feelings for long.)

Courtney's Antics

Courtney was a challenge to discipline. During the early stages of her life, her personality became evident. She was stubborn and prone to thinking up things that were "outside the box." Courtney had a way of using creativity, logic, and persuasion to talk us into giving her permission to do exactly what she wanted. Today, most of the frustrating incidents have drifted from my memory. Courtney was determined to live life on her own terms, not those of others. I was an only child who complied with my parents' expectations and was easily corrected (at least most of the time!). I expected Courtney to be just like me!

I took parenting classes that suggested the parent use "I" messages so the child would know how the parent feels. The clinical "reflecting" back on what the child said was useless. Courtney caught on. When I would read parenting books, they only made me feel incompetent and discouraged. I had a child who was totally impervious to such techniques! What I should have done in their place I did not know. Every other parent I knew seemed to have compliant children.

One day I came across an article in National Geographic. The author described how an octopus in a box would find its weakest point and get out. That was Courtney!

Courtney knew how to push my buttons. One day when she was in elementary school, she used the "f" word. I ignored it so as not to give too much importance to the word. After all, I had been trained in behavior modification so I knew what to do! She said it again. I sent her to her room. A few days later, she said it again. By this time I had had enough. I decided to use an old remedy! I took her to the bathroom to wash her mouth out with soap. Of course, she wouldn't open her mouth. Who would? Her little brother, Jason, was watching this scene and said to me, "You can't do that to my sister!" Although she escaped this ancient punishment, she never said that word again—at least in front of us!

One night John and I were out for the evening. My parents were visiting and in charge. Courtney had gone to bed apparently under much protest. My dad went to check on her and saw that she was "asleep." However, something told him to go back and take a closer look. She wasn't there! She had staged it to look as if she were asleep—complete with a pile of blankets and topped with a wig! I still remember feeling totally incredulous and stupefied. In retrospect, I admired her incredible creativity and slyness. I wouldn't have dreamed of doing anything like that when I was a child!

When she was in high school, Courtney, John, and I began family therapy—after all, we thought we must be doing something wrong. The therapist told us that Courtney was like an amoeba or cloud, constantly changing shape. Every time she thought she understood where Courtney was coming from, she would show another side of herself, which would change the direction of the process. She wasn't about to be defined or let others know who she really was. That described Courtney to a "T".

The therapist also made us aware that Courtney knew the limits of unacceptable behavior beyond which she would not go. "Yeah, right," I said to myself. I didn't understand what our therapist meant until Courtney told us she heard a friend swearing at her mother. I thought at the time, she does know her limits! She isn't so rebellious after all!

Courtney went to a high school that had an "open classroom" structure and curriculum. If you were late completing your homework, you would get a C when you handed in the assignment. That suited her just fine. Courtney had a way of assuring us that she had done her homework and was getting good grades, especially in January so she'd have her birthday parties or whatever before her grades came out!

After a choir trip to Russia, Courtney was behind in her homework and was not making an effort to complete it. It became clear that *she needed a school that provided more structure. Eventually, she transferred to a Quaker Friends school that had smaller class sizes. She thrived.*

College was a different story, as Courtney was neither ready nor interested. She had her own agenda. I know this is typical behavior for some kids this age. It seemed to us, however, that it was a continuation of her conflicting feelings about school. We finally stopped wasting our money and told her that when she was interested in going back to college, she would pay for the classes initially, and we would reimburse her if she got a C or better. We knew parents who had coronaries if their kids didn't get all A's! We would have been thrilled if she had just completed a class and gotten a C. I saw Courtney as a "late bloomer" and would, in all likelihood, go back to college when she was more mature.

When Courtney was in her twenties, she told me that we were good parents, particularly in disciplining her when she needed it. I laughed. I told her that we certainly didn't think so, as she always found a way to get around her punishments. If she couldn't watch TV, then she would read or listen to the radio, which was fine with her. Or if we took those away, she'd sit on her bed and make up stories in her head. Short of putting her in a straightjacket, we always felt we were not up to the task. Now, in retrospect, it comforts me to know that during those turbulent years, she knew we loved her and were there for her no matter what.

December 15, 2000

We attended Brian's commissioning ceremony here at Fort Benning, Georgia.

Some reflections on yesterday's ceremony:

It felt strange for two anti-Vietnam War protestors, such as John and me, to be going to an OCS graduation! When we walked past the tanks and cannons, I asked myself, *"How can this be?"* I said to John, "Isn't life strange, with all the twists and turns it takes?" The ceremony, of course, glorified the infantry from the Revolutionary War to the present. As the newly graduated men and women walked across the stage, looking so confident and impressive in their uniforms, I flashed on our friend John Chapman, who had died in Vietnam, and the multitude of other servicemen and women who died in that war. We were all thinking pretty much the same thing regarding the function of the infantry in war. We all prayed, to whomever listens, that Brian would stay out of harm's way until he would be accepted into medical school.

December 22, 2000

We're in River Falls *(our home town)* to spend Christmas with John's brother and family. It was very difficult to go to the cemetery where my parents and grandparents are buried. I had to dig down through the snow to uncover Grandpa and Grandma Armstrong's head-stone. I kept digging and crying until I uncovered all six of them. We scattered some of her ashes. I guess now that Courtney is gone, it magnifies my total loss. I had a good cry, and today I was able to keep myself together.

(In the past, before Courtney died, I would have feelings when I visited these graves of missing them and their stories of the past. I missed them but knew that their passing was the natural order of things. Our child had died before us. For me, that is one of the hardest things to get beyond and accept. I was numb at that time. As you

wind your way through this journey of grief, you may find yourself on a good day thinking you have accepted what has happened until the reality is repeated over and over again in unexpected ways.)

The "kids," our nephew and niece, were at my brother-in-law's tonight: Shannon, who is through with finals; Scott, Scott's wife Dani; and Jason. I don't know how I'll get through the next few days.

December 27, 2000

We made it through Christmas. It was difficult at the time, but the emphasis was on Christmas Eve: the gifts, dinner, and church service made it different. I managed to make it through the service and to sing all the carols.

John and his brother don't talk about Courtney. So we stick to mundane, irrelevant conversations for the most part.

One of John's cousins came over for dessert one evening. The conversation rambled until I asked her how long it had been since her son died. Then she and I talked about our deceased children. Her son called her the day he died to tell her he loved her. Even though John and I don't have a concrete incident like that from Courtney, she told us she loved us in many ways all the time.

We also talked to Brian. I had misplaced his number. I became very upset until Jason found it. Christmas day felt good and empty at the same time, but fortunately I snapped out of it once I talked to Brian. He is not sleeping well now that he is out of training and home on leave. Will this never end? We'll see him Friday.

Today is the thirty-fifth wedding anniversary for John and me. For now, some of the weight is lifting, and we're looking forward to dinner at the Lowell Inn and drinks at a friend's house. It doesn't seem that long ago! John and I have had a good life. I'm so lucky. His even temperament and sense of humor has gotten us through many a crisis.

January 2, 2001

We're back home. A real downer! Keeping a stiff upper lip for a week means you cry for a few days afterward! John and I both feel shell-shocked, bruised but hopeful that the New Year will be better. Could it be any worse?

We've been with Brian twice since we got back. It's great that he wants to be with us. He confessed last night that it was hard finding people to really talk to. He didn't want to upset us more by talking about Courtney. I told him we all needed to do just that. We're already upset! Brian told us that a young woman lost her husband in the spring while she was in OCS. He's been in contact with her.

Some interesting information came up from talking with Brian: Courtney didn't talk to him about her health and where it was going or where it might lead. She didn't want to upset us by talking to us about it either. Her anxiety was showing up in stomach problems.

January 8, 2001

John had a rough weekend with too much downtime. We reluctantly went to a friend's housewarming and managed to have a "good" time. Then we went to Center Stage to see three short plays by Thorton Wilder. I had no idea it would hit so close to home.

I remembered my reaction to *Our Town* twenty-five years ago. I couldn't stop crying when the young, pregnant wife died! At the time I didn't know why I was having such a reaction.

The second play, *The Long Christmas Dinner*, depicted a family over a ninety-year period. As time went on, the old ones, soldiers, and some children who had died were replaced by new family members who sat around the same dining room table. My dining room table is fifty-one years old. I remember my grandparents sitting at this table, and now there is the absence of Courtney. What a coincidence.

The last play, *Pullman Car Hiawatha*, was about a young woman who died of a heart attack on the train, and as the archangels assisted her into heaven, she said "good-bye" to everyone from her parents to her second grade teacher.

It was hard for us to stay in our seats and not run out of the theater screaming. John said he didn't need to see similar things like that now. My feeling is that we shouldn't avoid looking at them. If not now, then when? Courtney's death has really ripped him apart. I pray he stays well—me, too. John works with a woman who is a "psychic". She told him, and later me, that she had seen a woman in a Renaissance-style cape similar to the one we had given Courtney for Christmas. The woman asked Marie why she wasn't wearing Courtney's cape. The woman told Marie that Courtney wanted her to wear it. Apparently Sally can see spirits. She and I will talk more about this, perhaps. In the meantime I'm lighting candles and saying prayers.

January 10, 2001

A friend called to see how I was doing. She lost her son several years ago. It really helped to talk to her, one mother to another. Something weird: Courtney and my friend's son died in the same hospital. My friend and her husband had a lot of guilt surrounding his death. We don't go down that road—yet.

Brian called me last night. He misses talking to Courtney. So do I. I miss talking to her about theater, music, soap operas, ghosts, spirits, Wicca, and all the "weird stuff" in which she was interested. Brian went to close out Courtney's account at Social Security. That was hard for him. I think he finds it hard to talk about Courtney and his feelings. We're at the stage where no one wants to bring "It" up because they don't want to upset us.

January 14, 2001

It's interesting—which is a poor word—how grief lies low for a few days, maybe even a week, and then "bubbles up" like a vessel full to overflowing. I couldn't sleep much last night, thinking about business transactions and wondering how those will come out, and of course, Courtney. By this morning I found myself still ruminating, and tears were close to the surface. The realization of It is too much. I heard a woman talk about how proud she was of her daughter studying for her PhD. Why couldn't Courtney have had just one baby? Why did this have to happen to our daughter? Why were we chosen? Etc. Etc. Etc....

January 21, 2001

Courtney's twenty-ninth birthday! Twenty-nine years ago, I was higher than a kite with a beautiful little girl. Two days later, we started our journey of hospitals, EKGs, cardiac catheterizations, dance and piano lessons, make-believe, travel, books, vampires, witches, cats, wolves, big sister, and spouse.

Courtney's Birth and Surgery

I did not write in a journal after Courtney's birth. I remember feeling that if I wrote it down, it would be real. After all, the story wasn't supposed to be like this. I wrote nothing. I have no notes about this early time. I felt if I returned her to my womb I could keep her safe. I did not keep a journal during her pre-surgery, surgery and post surgery. I am writing now from memory.

On January 21, 1972, Courtney Baker was born in Lawrence, Kansas. I had an uneventful pregnancy filled with excitement and awe at the various changes in my body and of the baby growing inside me. John and I took the Lamaze childbirth classes, and I joined La Leche League. After a "normal" labor and delivery, Courtney Baker was born! It was the high point of my life! I was totally present for this miracle unfolding before my eyes.

Courtney was six pounds, thirteen ounces and twenty inches long. Her color was normal and she was very alert. The initial nursing was as it should be. However, as time went on, Courtney began to have difficulty coordinating her breathing with nursing. I wasn't terribly concerned as I had read that it took a few days for a baby to adjust. My parents called the next morning. My mother wanted to know the baby's color. I thought at the time that it was a peculiar question for a first time grandmother to ask. I said that she was kind of a bluish. My mother said later that an electric shock went through her. I sensed her concern and told her that, from what I had read, some newborns took awhile to pink up.

I soon became uneasy and felt something was wrong. However, every time I saw her, I felt her strength, and I believed that everything was going to be all right.

On Friday, January 22, 1972, as Courtney was having more and more trouble breathing, Dr. Margaret, my GP, called in a pediatrician to take a look at her. He could not determine the problem. The pediatrician recommended transporting her to the University of Kansas Medical Center in Kansas City. John, who had been by my side continuously, followed the ambulance to the hospital. A longtime friend met John at the hospital and stayed with him during the testing.

Mothers weren't discharged that quickly in those days, so I was left behind. I was like a mother bear without her cub and had to be sedated. Another friend lent her calming presence and stayed with me that day. John called eventually to tell me that the hole that naturally stays open after birth was closing depriving her of oxygen. They were going to do a procedure that had a fifty-fifty chance of success. I can't remember how I responded that day; everything was so surreal. About an hour and a half later, John called to tell me that the procedure had been a success. The cardiologist had inserted a catheter into a vein in her groin and then fed it carefully into her heart to create a new hole to replace the one that was closing.

One of the doctors told John, "She is a very strong baby." The bad news: she had a congenital heart defect called Transposition of the Great Vessels. This meant that the pulmonary artery and aorta had not crossed during the first few weeks of development. The arteries were parallel.

The next day I was released from the hospital, and John drove me to Kansas City to the medical center. When I first saw Courtney, she was in an incubator attached to monitors. An Indian pediatrician introduced himself and asked me if I wanted to nurse her. Of course! When he observed that Courtney had no trouble, he told us the cardiologists did not recommend that I nurse her. They felt it would be too difficult and strenuous for her and would put a strain on her heart. He told them, where he came from, mother's milk was the best thing for a baby and encouraged me to continue nursing her. I felt so helpless! I was convinced that nursing was the only thing I could do for her and would have fought the doctors. The hospital had hotel-style rooms for parents whose babies were in the neo-natal intensive care unit. I nursed her around the clock.

Another concern at that time was the medical expenses. John was completing his degree, and I had a job that covered our living expenses but no more. The doctor put us in touch with the Crippled Children's Foundation. I think that was the only foundation that was funding children with any kind of defect at the time. We completed the necessary paperwork and were accepted very quickly. Friends came and picked us up and brought us home. All of this took place within five days from the day she was born.

In looking back on this experience, we didn't know what we didn't know. We knew that she had a serious congenital heart defect that would be corrected by open heart surgery at some point in the future. John and I were just so happy that Courtney had lived! I always felt, from the day she was born, that she had tremendous strength and determination. Every time I looked at her, I put any worries aside. We were simply typical new parents adjusting to late nights, diapering, nursing, etc. All our friends told us she was a beautiful baby! They brought food, gifts, and themselves to support us.

Some people have a way of not thinking before they say something. I remember the first time I cried. A neighbor asked me when was I going to start Courtney on cereal. I told her in five or six months (La Leche recommended). She said, with grave concern, "You know what's going to happen, don't you?" I was suddenly alarmed and scared. What more could possibly happen or be worse than what we had already been through? I said, "What's going to happen?!" She answered, "The baby won't be able to use her spoon!" I was stunned and didn't know what to say. I finally said to her, "If Courtney is using a spoon by the time she goes to kindergarten, I'll be happy!" With that, my neighbor left in a huff. That was the final straw! I immediately burst into tears.

By June, Courtney was not gaining much weight. When we were in Wisconsin, a friend of my mother's said to me that my milk must not be very rich since Courtney was so small! We were asked many times if we knew our baby was blue!

The next few months were filled with doctors' appointments, excitement over putting college behind us, and going back home to see our parents before we drove to Virginia for John's first job. The doctors were pleased with Courtney's progress, although she became blue around her mouth and nose when she cried. We became accustomed to it and didn't worry. The pediatric cardiologist had told me that if her respiration increased to a certain level, I was to immediately bring her in to be checked. I soon realized that if I focused on counting her breaths, I would make myself crazy, and Courtney, too! Again, we didn't know what we didn't know—thank goodness! She was our baby, and we had no other child with whom to compare her.

UNSPEAKABLE!

It was prior to our leaving Lawrence that John and I began to exhibit stress reactions. One evening, just after we brought Courtney home, John walked over to Allen Field House to watch a KU basketball game. He slipped and fell. He didn't think anything about it until he realized that his legs were like rubber, and he fell again and again. He finally got to the game and sat there as if he were behind some kind of barrier.

Since high school, I've always suffered from dermatitis during stressful situations. This time I began to develop welts on my feet and hands. Nothing I put on topically did any good. I didn't realize that although I was excited about leaving Kansas, going home to Wisconsin, and then on to Virginia, I was having a severe reaction to all the stress since Courtney's birth. After we arrived in our hometown, I went to our family doctor, who gave me a shot of ACTH, adrenocorticotrophic hormone. It immediately *stopped the itching and calmed me down.*

We saw a pediatric cardiologist at the University of Virginia. By this time Courtney was only gaining 1.25 pounds every two months. We were told that it would be two years or twenty pounds before they could do open heart surgery. That was an eternity for us! Somehow I put it in the back of my mind in between appointments and was able to enjoy being a new mother.

The reality of the severity of Courtney's condition came in August 1972. Fortunately, a friend drove me to the appointment. Prior to this, John and I were positive that Courtney had gained weight. Of course the first thing the nurse did was weigh her. She had not gained anything! What a shock! What would happen now? Was she going to die? What were the doctors going to do? I went into a meltdown! I couldn't stop crying. After that, my anxiety would spike periodically—especially if I were in a play group with other mothers. I finally avoided such groups, as it was very obvious that

Courtney wasn't gaining weight nor keeping up developmentally with her peers. I would call John when I had an anxiety attack. He would leave work and take care of Courtney while I went out for a couple of hours.

By Fall Courtney could sit up, play with her toys and look at books and magazines. She had the ability to turn each page very carefully, without ripping the pages as other babies did. She was very alert and watched everything with great interest. Although we talked to her incessantly, she did not babble nor try to imitate us until after her surgery. When Courtney and I went to her next appointment in October, John came with us. At that time there was little change in her weight. The situation to us seemed endless. At our December appointment, the cardiologists told us unexpectedly that Courtney needed to have open heart surgery in the next few months. They were not going to wait until she was twenty pounds or two years old as they had initially told us. We later learned that a baby with the same defect, also named Courtney, had died in December. The surgery was set for March 20, 1973.

Courtney's grandparents were very supportive, sending care packages and calling us often. My father-in-law would occasionally blame his side of the family for causing her heart defect. Our doctors continued to insist that her condition was not hereditary. Whatever strong emotions our parents had regarding Courtney's pending surgery, we did not see or hear of them. Everyone kept a positive attitude. My parents especially behaved just like grandparents with their first grandchild. I was actually relieved when they were unable to see Courtney during the five weeks of her hospitalization. It would have taken more energy for me to keep a stiff upper lip.

John took a picture of Courtney and me the day we took her to the hospital for her surgery. I had been crying. I can still feel the dispair and fear of those days. The future was impossible to predict—almost like a bad soap opera: tune in tomorrow. I remember thinking, as I was bathing her before we left for the hospital, "Why do we need to do this? She seems fine right now." I couldn't bear to think of her being cut open!

The night before her surgery, we kissed her good night, not knowing whether we would ever see her alive again. It was the most frightening night of our lives!

The next day, the surgeon told us the surgery would take a couple of hours, which turned out to be four. While sitting in the waiting room, I began to smell BO. I looked around at the people sitting closest to us. Then I looked at John. He was sweating so much his shirt was soaked! Finally, it was over. The surgery had been successful! Courtney was awake and alert. However, in those days, the parents weren't allowed to see their children until the next day. The surgeon told us to get out of the hospital, have dinner, and go to a movie. That was very good advice.

In the morning we were led into the pediatric ICU. Courtney wouldn't look at us. The staff said that many babies will not look at their parents for a few days after surgery, as if to say, "How could you do this to me?" John and I were not upset. It was just so good to see her alive and pink! It was finally over, and she was pink!

January 21, 2001, continued

A few days before Courtney's birthday, John returned from Moscow. (*He worked at the Department of Energy and flew to Moscow from time to time.*) He told me about his latest dream. Courtney was leaving for St. Louis. When John gave her a kiss, she was crying because she knew she wasn't coming back.

Today we awoke to a gloriously beautiful day—four inches of snow, trees laden with a light white cover, and a clear blue sky so like the day Courtney was born. We had bought a bouquet of sunflowers, white carnations, and daisies for the altar at church. A woman called to tell us that services had been cancelled because of the weather. A typical Maryland response to a few inches of snow! I had planned on lighting a candle for Courtney and was hoping I could do it. We had bagels with our friends, as usual, and they invited us for dinner.

Around noon, we drove down to the National Zoo. Courtney loved the zoo! I hadn't been there since Jason was in middle school. I wanted to do something Courtney would have done: see the new pandas! They were sleeping the first time we saw them. When we came back a few minutes later, they were eating bamboo, climbing a tree, and hanging from a limb!

Later, at our friend's house, we talked about Courtney, spirits, visions, and my friend's ability to see spirits and have lucid dreams. I think John had a hard time intellectually with the discussion but also emotionally, since he was having lucid dreams about Courtney. This was the first time we'd talked to anyone like this.

We also laughed. My friend told stories about her childhood when she imitated the rabbi and got thrown out of Hebrew school! Then I had to tell my stories. It felt so good to laugh! I never dreamed that I'd be laughing, today of all days.

I have suggested to John and Jason that for Courtney's future birthdays, I'll make her favorite dinner every year on her birthday: Country Captain, her favorite chicken dish, and rum cake.

UNSPEAKABLE!

February 1, 2001

Today a customer asked me about my children. I said I had two: a son who lived nearby and a daughter who had passed. She asked when. Afterward it was business as usual, and we went on with the appointment. My customer has a little girl named Hannah Elizabeth, just like Grandma Mac!

At noon I had lunch with a friend. We talked about Courtney, her sister, and her niece, who had passed. Then I went to Produce Galore and ran into four people I knew—all except one knew about Courtney. By the time I got home, I was in tears and exhausted. Making Courtney's birthday dinner with Jason and having John home eased the pain.

Jason is home after visiting his girl friend in Eastern Russia. John is home from Moscow. Jason told us that Courtney was in his thoughts on the twenty-first. I said a "Meta" prayer before we toasted her:

"May all beings be happy.

May all beings be healed and whole again.

May we have what we want and need.

May we be protected from harm and free from fear.

May we become enlightened, liberated, and free.

May we enjoy inner peace and ease.

May there peace in the world."

We leave on the third for Vancouver to meet our friends from

California for a week of skiing. My cousin and her husband will join us. We are truly blessed.

February 14, 2001

My first Valentine's Day without Courtney. *(I found a Valentine card from her while I was transcribing this journal. She was living in Florida at the time. I could hear her voice as I read it.)*

Mom and Dad,

Thanks for all your help. I love you always and miss you a lot! Happy Valentine's Day!

Love,

Your Daughter

February 16, 2001

We've been home for almost a week. We had a glorious, exhausting time skiing, as well as a lot of fun. It was good to be with our friends and cousins. John mentioned Courtney a couple of times, but it was when I was alone with my friend Mary and my cousin Susie that I talked about her death. I wanted to spend more time with them, but there seems like there is never enough time. It was so good to be able to open up. My friend is worried about John and me. She has an inkling of what it must be like, but parents don't really know until it happens to them. To lose a child, no one wants that!

UNSPEAKABLE!

I guess what I've been feeling this week is that we will never be the same. We will always be on the outside looking in. The pain will lessen, but it will never go away—and every pleasant moment, event, trip, or outing with friends or family is only a brief diversion from the pain of her loss.

February 27, 2001

It's been six months to the day since Courtney died. As I write the word "died," I still can't believe it happened! At times I feel hollow—nothing but hard acceptance. Then something will bring it up again—a memory, a person—and the tears will come. Today everything is setting me off.

Jason is in Massachusetts at Kripalu for three months. John, fortunately, is not traveling. Brian is still in training. I'm afraid of the future. Are we all going to come together stronger than we were before Courtney died? Or are we going to be these separate entities in our own little worlds? Maybe it's a combination. I can't dwell on it or be afraid, but it's there.

I have no dreams of Courtney. No sign of her presence except when she's in my thoughts. It's all a waiting game now.

March 6, 2001

I leave for Kripalu tomorrow. I drew the "Wisdom" card from the *Power Deck* with a picture of a snow-covered pagoda. The definition is that wisdom comes from the north, and I'm going north to lots of snow in Massachusetts!

My work has picked up, and I'm very busy and focused. It helps to feel that my energy is back.

March 8, 2001

I've had one full day at Kripalu among the Berkshires in Massachusetts. I've done yoga twice and had a massage! In the morning, there was a sharing circle, and of course when it became my turn, I had a difficult time sharing my reasons/feelings about being there.

The whole atmosphere here is one of calm, quiet acceptance. They don't even have locks on the doors to the rooms. I thought I'd have a hard time sleeping, but I didn't. The food is all vegetarian and absolutely delicious! I look forward to every meal. My meditation program starts tonight.

March 11, 2001

Where do I begin? I've had a profound weekend and an even more profound day!

I had a wonderful weekend of mostly silence. A friend from grade school called to wish me a happy birthday. She couldn't believe I had been *silent* for most of the weekend! I spoke mostly to Jason. Kripalu is truly a wonderful place to get away from this crazy pace we set for ourselves. The food was fabulous! I did the dance kinetics class twice. Basically, it's dancing free form or following a leader to music or live drumming. I had many experiences, but I lost it when I realized I was in a room full of twenty year olds. Courtney should be reveling here, not her fifty-six year old mother! No answer. No answer for tonight either.

The chanting we did was awesome; the walking meditation was interesting, and so was the conscious eating experience. But the silence was best of all: no talking at breakfast. It was great! I love the yoga, both "gentle" and "moderate." It really helped to fine-tune what I have been doing and to reinforce what my yoga practice is about. I feel I need to do some of that before meditation every day. Wow! The older I get, the more I don't know and yet...

This was my first birthday without Courtney in twenty-nine years. John picked me up at the airport and took me to dinner at our favorite restaurant in Baltimore: Boccocio's. While we were having dinner, a man at a table nearby collapsed with cardiac arrest. A doctor in the restaurant worked on him, the ambulance came. He was breathing, we think, when he was taken away. Hasn't life taught us that we are all held by a thin thread? Yet we have to be reminded of it over and over.

My digestion stopped, and I began to shake when all this was happening. I went to the ladies' room, and while there I said the Meta prayer. I was shaking uncontrollably while I was saying the prayer. A little over twenty-four hours ago, my instructor at Kripalu talked about the various people for whom to say that prayer. She said one of them should be a person about whom you felt neutral. This man must be an example!

Courtney's last birthday card to me.

Mom,

Hope you remember your dreams and can write them down in this book. Thank you for putting up with me through this time period in my life.

Happy Birthday.

Hope this helps. (She gave me a journal for my birthday. I did not write in it until after she died.)

March 31, 2001, 12:30 a.m.

This month has been a full one: Kripalu, my birthday, my best month ever in real estate!

Work is essential now. When I'm not working (and this goes for John, too), the grief washes over me. When we see a young woman with a baby, when we remember Courtney's voice, or when the phone rings, it's still unbearable—but work helps.

Today a couple of strange things happened. I had a message on my voice mail. It was music. I waited for a voice to come on, and then I heard: "From a Distance." I started to cry. Was this a joke, coincidence, or something else? I came home and John showed me what had come to us by fax, something about Armageddon.

April 2, 2001

I saw a baby today. Another realtor brought her new grandson in and stopped by my office. I don't think anyone remembers that Courtney was almost four months pregnant when she died. The baby was eight weeks and beautiful: lots of blond hair and blue eyes. He could have been Brian and Courtney's baby. Oh, the pain! I managed to get the rest of my work done and then got out of there. This is how it's going to be. Unexpected encounters, then the pain, the reality of the loss, then blow your nose and go on—somehow.

April 6, 2001

It's amazing how John and I can go about our everyday lives and, to the outside world, look and act normal. Tears are always near, but work keeps them at bay. John has trouble on weekends. Our worst day is Sunday. The silence is unbearable. No dreams of her, no signs of any kind—nothing. We were both crying after watching the movie *Nell*. John was crying because of the little girl at the end, and I was crying because Nell was always grieving for her dead sister. This pain will never end!

April 15, 2001

It's Easter. Our minister gave a beautiful sermon about hope and resurrection from bad life experiences. I was doing OK until she read a poem about moving through the pain into the light. We're not there yet. I had to leave during the last hymn. There is no hope for us.

April 30, 2001

We have a date for interring Courtney's ashes. This is so hard for me. It has to be done. It will be June 10— just family and roses at Arlington National Cemetery.

While I was drying my hair, these words—the beginning of something—came to me. I want to write them down before I forget:

Once, a long time ago, you were a part of me.

Once, a long time ago, I nurtured you within my body.

Once, a long time ago, I protected you from all harm and you were safe.

When you were born, our bodies separated, and we became mother and daughter.

I could not protect you.

It was then, a long time ago, I asked a favor to keep you, at least for a while.

May 12, 2001

John and I are at Kripalu for Mother's Day weekend and Jason's birthday. Time is different up here. There are so many experiences squeezed into a few days, it seems as though we've been here longer. I participated in a mind-body workshop yesterday. The leader asked us to rate our stress level. She read a poem by Rumi who said something about welcoming travail and grief into your home for

47

personal and spiritual growth will follow. Courtney's death was the impetus for making my first reservation here. What other doors? What is next for me?

I participated in a guided meditation. We visualized the chakra colors. When it ended, we were asked to write down what we saw, felt, and sensed in that space between the exhalation and inhalation. I thought, *Oh no, what am I going to write?* I saw, felt, and sensed nothing.

Somehow I wrote the following:

Out of nowhere into nowhere

Out of color into emptiness

Out of warmth into coolness

Out of height into depth

Out of stable into unstable

I had never really thought about that space before. I'll look there again.

John and I went for a walk with Jason up to a pond and sat and talked a while. I told him it was very difficult for me right now: Mother's Day, and planning the interment. I don't think he understands, nor can he. He sees it as a celebration, but he listens...

Jason is looking more like an ascetic priest or some holy man! People here even say he seems like a priest. (An old friend said that, too.) John just shakes his head!

John has walked in the woods while we've been here. No yoga for him. We're going this morning for a long walk again. I had a Reiki treatment yesterday. It's basically the laying on of hands, with the practitioner being an instrument or conduit. She called angels and my guides to be there, and then she began. I felt heat, color, and deep relaxation. She wants me to call her when I get a chest X-ray, since I'm having trouble with my feet in that area (a reflexology treatment confirmed that) and my acupuncturist is treating me in the lung area. Also she recommended a combination of reflexology and Reiki. Of course she emphasized taking care of myself during this time.

June 4, 2001

I'm tired of coping! I'm sick of being strong and "doing so well." I picked up Courtney's ashes at Witzkes Funeral Home. A friend went with me to Arlington so Courtney's ashes can be buried. Ordeal after ordeal! A woman I know who lost her eighteen-year-old son a few years ago said, "It will get better." Ha!

Brian called this morning. He's here on leave. He faxed the necessary paperwork to Arlington. He said, "We got here around midnight," and then told me that "Jen" was here with him. He met her at a friend's wedding. She's leaving Thursday, but he'll be showing her around Maryland for a few days while staying at his father's.

I knew eventually this would happen—of course, he's young. But I keep thinking: *Not now, not this week!* I feel like I'm losing everything—Courtney, now Brian. I've got to be careful so I don't upset him. He deserves to be happy and find someone else.

UNSPEAKABLE!

June 5, 2001

So many emotions are going through my mind. I feel as though we're being punished, especially when I see other people with or talking about their children and grandchildren. I also feel guilty that, being Courtney's mother, Brian bit off a lot marrying her. I guess I feel guilty for the pain I've caused him or, more realistically, the pain he's going through.

Another friend called this morning, and I told her about Jen. She feels that it was going to happen sooner or later, but that it's happening this week will simply push us to face the inevitable. It's unbelievably painful. It's tough. It continues to be tough.

June 25, 2001

It's been several days since I felt the need to write. Usually that means an easing up from the constant pain. This time I've just been busy and avoiding my journal.

After Jen left, Brian came over to the house. We saw him every day until he left on the eleventh. We had many good talks, and I was able to let him know we support him in whatever he does. We spent several days planning the interment service. We were upset when we found out that Courtney's ashes were put in the "columbarium" instead of buried.

The service was at the columbarium. I gave everyone a rose. We stood in a circle and shared our thoughts and remembrances of Courtney. I read the poem I began on April 30:

For Courtney

Once, a long time ago, you were a part of me.

Once, a long time ago, I nurtured you within my body

I protected you from all harm.

You were safe.

A long time ago, and yet it seems like yesterday,

you entered this world.

We, you and I, became separate beings.

There was no protection.

It was then I asked a favor: to keep you for a little while

For Parties

For Halloween

For Travels with Pop and Nana.

To become a Big Sister

For Friends

For Romance

UNSPEAKABLE!

For Marriage

For Motherhood

For Love.

And now it has come to pass.

What you knew and I knew:

Your story to end before mine.

What now?

How do I go on?

What door will open in your wake?

Time only time...

Brain and Courtney's friends said or read something; Brian's brother and stepfather shared, too. Somehow it was a relief to have it over.

Yesterday my friend from Wheeling stayed overnight. She was in the area to pick up a car in Fairfax. We drove to Arlington National Cemetery to see whether Courtney's ashes had been moved. They had, and they are now at the corner of Bradley and Patton: 70-1697. Her stone will be ready in September.

John and I had a long talk after he came home from Russia. I told him all of the darkest feelings that take hold sometimes: the feeling of being punished, the feeling of despair, the feeling of further calamities awaiting us, the feeling that my life is over. He listened, tried to reason with me in his usual fashion, but emphasized that he wanted me to talk to him about these fears and feelings and not keep them to myself.

What a continuing horror!

Prayers for Brian this week during paratrooper school.

July 4, 2001

We had ten people for a rainy barbecue. It was a great group of people. Lots of spiritual energy! Six months ago, I wouldn't have had the energy to pull this off. Somehow my energy is back.

I dreamed of Courtney last night. She was standing with a black, eye patch on. I think she took it off. I started shaking and crying. My sister-in-law and niece were with me, and I remember thinking as we went into this church that soon they would be experiencing a loss. Did C's mask mean that she now could "see"—that the blinders had come off? Or was it that I couldn't see her with the mask on?

UNSPEAKABLE!

July 16, 2001

I'm angry! I have no control over life! I'm angry at Courtney for putting me through 28½ years of turmoil, anxiety, stubbornness, and doing what she wanted to regardless of the consequences!

I'm angry at Jason for tilting at windmills without sufficient planning! Now he's going off to Russia, again, with a couple thousand dollars in his pocket and in August of all months!

I'm angry with John for not talking about Courtney and then telling me when I get teary to "not get started"! He retreats to the TV and can watch hours and hours of it!

I'm angry that I have to cope daily with a spectrum of emotions and, at the same time, exhibit infinite patience with my clients! And then there is the computer, the web, the myriad of techno speak, and the prodding to get this or that upgrade. I'm angry over the time it takes to coordinate and understand it all—and for what!?

I feel better. Whew!

Later—

I'm so tired. Came home after an appointment was canceled. I'm so grateful for the business I've had, but I'm also worn out. I miss Courtney. I miss talking to her about all kinds of things. I miss worrying about her and getting irritated. Now it's just Jason. He's feeling the full amount of "parenting" that was diluted when C was alive. A year ago we were worrying about her. Now Jason gets it all!

July 27, 2001

It's been eleven months to the day that Courtney died. Brian left today for Fort Lewis and to pick up his girlfriend in Indiana. She is moving out there with him and has two job offers. Jason is leaving the sixteenth for Russia. I just got back from having a root canal. There was a call from a friend telling me she lost her thirty-seven-year-old son on Sunday from a freak accident. Now another mother and father grieving! I know the above is just life doing what life does, but I've had enough. I'm tired. I've been beaten up, overworked, and I need a rest.

August 3, 2001

Nothing has changed. Instead of a weekend off, I'm showing property. At least my clients are a pleasure to be with.

I've been more or less awake since 2:30 a.m. Saw *Peggy Sue Got Married* again. Neat movie. John is on his way to Russia for a week. Jason is off; I don't know where. He could have called!

I can't worry. I need sleep. I have to be ready and accept what life will deal me next. I miss Courtney so much.

August 6, 2001

A year ago, I went with Courtney to her OB appointment and heard the baby's heartbeat. I didn't dare get excited about becoming a grandmother. It was a long time until February, when her baby would have been born. This month will be tough, but somehow

55

with my real estate responsibilities, I don't have a lot of time to dwell. Brian is in Washington state. Jason is waiting for his visa to return to Russia...a year has almost passed. I can't believe it. I asked "Whomever" what was I to do now? I pulled a rune stone that is called "New Beginnings." That certainly is true for Brian and Jason. What about John and me? It says that we will emerge from a "chrysalis-like state"—a release that would ease tension and uncertainty. From this, we would become centered and grounded.

The pain is still there, while at the same time, there is happiness in helping Jason design an engagement ring for his fiancé.

August 21, 2001

Six days before the anniversary of Courtney's death! We've been grieving fifty-one weeks. Instead of shock, horror, and raw, unrelenting pain, it's now dull, unrelenting pain. We can go through the motions in the company of others—and it's a relief for a while. I get in my car to go shopping or to an appointment, and then "It" slips in.

Jason will leave Thursday the twenty-third, the same day we leave for Rockport, Massachusetts. Susan, his fiancée, is anxious to see him, and he's anxious to see her and get on with his life. What do we do? I'm sure we'll think of something. Sometimes I feel old and that we are the only ones "holding the bag." Sometimes I feel Courtney is far away from us now. The only way to feel close to her is to hang on to the day she died. Yet sometimes I feel her close by. But I don't like this veil separating us—making me guess, imagine, hope, but not easily communicate.

A friend lost her husband to a heart attack two weeks ago. Now she is going through the challenge of grief, too. I'm tired, exhausted from these past fifty-one weeks. How do I live the rest of my life?

August 24, 2001

How can I forget what month this is? We're in Rockport, Massachusetts. I'm sitting, doing nothing: reading, sleeping, and watching the seagulls. I feel as if I'm recovering from a long illness or major surgery. I'm perfectly content to sit here and not talk, even to John. Whatever is here is healing: the wind; the water; the trees. The shops in town are overwhelming with their abundance of items to buy. None of it interests me.

Jason is somewhere between Alaska and Seoul, South Korea. He will call John's voice mail and leave a message. It was hard saying good-bye, but we all did it and hoped for the best. We are held here by such a thin thread. I'm shell-shocked. I know anything can happen at any time. The trick is making the best of your time—yes, even having fun while you're watching and waiting.

I talked to one of Courtney's close friends last Sunday. Courtney told her, the April before she died, that if something happened to her, Brian should get on with his life whether it was three months or three years later. Brian is out at Fort Lewis with Jen. I'm numb but I'll be ready to meet her when the time comes.

CHAPTER 2

Anger!

August 28, 2001

We had a relaxing but sad time in Rockport. The twenty-seventh came and went—no better or worse than any other day since Courtney died. Even today, as I write those words, I can't believe it's real!

John had a harder time than I did. He had another one of his dreams yesterday morning, right before he woke up. A two-year-old was bouncing on the bed and holding her arms out to him. He said, "Come to Daddy" or "Give Daddy a hug." The little girl gave him a hug that felt more like a hug from an adult. He woke up—at first happy, then upset, when he realized what it was...a dream.

September 10, 2001

I'm in Ocean City at the MAR (Maryland Association of Realtors) conference. I treated myself to the Dunes Hotel and what a treat! I have a quiet, oceanfront room. A storm is coming in as I write this on the deck. I could have stayed with two other women, but I need and crave the peace and quiet. I was in class all day. I saw people I knew. That was enough.

I went to a friend's temporary digs, saw their almost-completed new home, and went out for dinner. Their son Steven's death was two months ago. I'm over a year away, and it's still so painful. They have a new house and a new grandchild to look forward to. We can't escape the reality no matter what we do to divert ourselves. We have to go on—how, I don't know.

We're not like anyone else. I'm so consumed with my grief that I find it hard to make small talk—although I don't know if anyone notices! I skipped two cocktail parties just for that reason. I'll go to the dinner tomorrow night to support my friends, who will be honored, but that's it. I'll arrive a half hour before dinner so I don't have to stand around too long and schmooze!

Hollowness, panic, and shock are still with me. We dress up, go through the motions. I must be repeating myself, but it keeps going on and on. There will be no end.

September 17, 2001

September 11 came with an unspeakable bang. The World Trade Center and the Pentagon were attacked—thousands killed by terrorists! My grief is now magnified and repeated a thousand fold! It's been hard to make sense of it all, to realize that this is not a bad dream but something really happened.

After the Pentagon was hit, I couldn't get in touch with John who was working in D.C. There were rumors that there were fires on the Mall. The MAR conference was canceled. I returned to the hotel and went to the beach to wait. At 3:00 p.m., John got through. It had taken him three hours to get home. We don't know what will come next! Other planes down? Bombs going off? John thinks I'm being "fatalistic." I have felt for a long time—even before the eleventh—that we're held by a thin thread; nothing is guaranteed. In my darkest moments, I feel that if we happened to die by whatever means, at least the pain would be over and just maybe we would see Courtney again. This mortal plane is a tough one.

Brian is "safe" for the time being. His unit is not ready to be deployed for another eighteen months and fortunately will serve the Asian conflicts. He called immediately Tuesday when he heard about the Pentagon to see how John was.

John and I went to the cemetery Saturday. Still no stone. They had Sections 69 and 70 cordoned off because those sections were close to the Pentagon. We put sunflowers on Courtney's grave. Then I took a picture of the damage done to the Pentagon.

The horror—our horror—pales in comparison to what the victims experienced the last moments of their lives. You can feel the pain left behind.

October 23, 2001

I can't believe it's been over a month since I wrote in this book! Since then we took an unexpected trip to Vienna, Austria. What a wonderful city! What a wonderful diversion!

Courtney's stone is finally in place. John went over to the cemetery last week and saw it. Another milestone along our pathway of grief! We e-mailed Brian to let him know. He called last night to talk about any changes he may want to make to it. He wants John to take a picture of it and send it to him. He won't be home for Christmas due to the current state of affairs. It sounds as though he is being trained to be deployed if needed inside the country. I'm glad he is where he is.

Jason is having an adventure in Russia, complete with a radio show! However, he, too, is having lucid dreams. His last dream was of Courtney being with us at a party holding a glass of rum and Coke with a plate of food. She never ate or drank any of it. Jason feels that the dream meant she was with us but in a different form.

I sometimes think messages from somewhere come through during meditation, but I'm not sure. My feelings are right underneath the surface. John doesn't want to talk about "It"—Courtney, her death, the aftermath—because we've talked about "It " before. His repeating mantra is "It doesn't make any difference." We're both dealing with Courtney's death (fourteen months out) differently. We both agree that we will never be over "It" or feel "better" about "It."

One of my spiritual friends gave me the phone number and website address of a psychic. I haven't been eager to call her, as most of the readings seem like parlor games. I want to grow and explore more spiritual and psychic techniques to connect with Courtney. I've always been interested in readings and hearing about the experiences of others. It just doesn't happen to me. I'm still coping with living without her—we all are.

John is so closed off. He keeps putting on weight and then losing a couple of pounds. From my perspective, he is doing *nothing* to prevent a future disaster health-wise. I asked him if he was deliberately trying to cause something. He wouldn't give me a straight answer and is angry at me for pointing out the amount of fat he consumes.

I guess we are just plain angry about everything! It's an empty feeling sometimes. We have the little respites: Vienna, Jason coming home for Christmas, skiing. In between we have the arduous task of living day to day. Upon reflection of that last sentence, it may not be that bleak—there *is* laughter, humor, and many pleasant moments. I try to pay attention...

October 27, 2001

Today we planted a white dogwood "Navaho Princess" with a portion of Courtney's ashes. This was not planned, as I didn't know when the tree was going to be delivered. Our landscaper didn't call until Thursday or Friday. Everything came together today.

How much more must I endure? We dug the hole. I put a few of Courtney's ashes in it before we planted the tree. The bone fragments among the ashes are unbearable to see! I still go on, I breathe, I take plants in for the winter, I rake leaves; I get dressed up and go out to dinner. How can this be? How does life go on? How do I continue to exist?

October 30, 2001

I met a career coach who spoke at the Business Women's Network. I'm going to work with her on business goals and redefining reality. She may help me go deeper, as I think that is where the next step is. She told me, after I described Courtney and my loss, that "It is a privilege to talk to you today." She felt I was doing everything I could, i.e., exercise, meditation, yoga, etc. She also mentioned that the second year of grief is a different ball game and that not much has been written about it. It was good to hear that feedback.

November 12, 2001

Another plane crash, but authorities are not suspecting terrorists. All the grief in the world tonight—every night: the shock, the disbelief, the anguish, the ache in your heart that will never end. We sang "Danny Boy" yesterday at church. I don't know how I got through it.

Buddha says one needs to accept death before one can truly live. It's easier intellectually but not when you are doubled over with the pain. Am I mourning Courtney, myself, or both at the same time? I don't know. Sometimes I'm so filled with loss, regret, and at times guilt, I can't move. It doesn't last long, and I continue to push myself along.

Why don't I dream about her? Why doesn't she talk to me in my dreams or even appear? She and I talked about all of these things when she was alive, but now there is nothing. Maybe because there *is* nothing, a void into which we all go.

Courtney saw her guardian angel several times but always referred to her as "The Lady" or, at first, a ghost. It wasn't until a week before she died that she referred to her as her guardian angel! When I think of her, her essence, her sense of humor, her quirkiness, I get this overwhelming sense of loss. We miss her so much. How are we to live the remaining years of our lives? The other night, I saw a friend who is eighty something. Thirty more years—maybe—with this pain. My baby has been taken from me, and her baby, too!

November 15, 2001

I've started reading George Anderson's book *Walking in the Garden of Souls*. He wrote about his ability to communicate with the dead.

UNSPEAKABLE!

Apparently, he's had this ability all of his life.

As I was fixing dinner for myself, I started to imagine what I would say to Courtney if I had the chance to talk to her. I started to cry and became angry. I was talking out loud and asking, "What were you thinking?! Why didn't you go to the emergency room? You always thought you knew everything! You didn't know enough—you made sure of that when you chose not to study and go to college."

I'm afraid it would not be pleasant. I've been angry a long time but have been too consumed with grief and shock to fully feel it. Now it's finally coming to the surface. Her whole life I tried to encourage her to control what she could control. Education was my main concern. From fifth grade on, she took the easy way out. Because she knew a little bit but not enough, she died and the baby died with her. How could she do that to herself, the baby, to Brian, and to us?

None of this makes sense because it may have been worse as the pregnancy went on. But the feeling, the resentment, for having caused us pain is there. John will think this unnecessary: "Why go there? What difference does it make?" But those feelings are there. The resentment, the feeling of failure as a parent when it came to raising her—they are all there. Maybe by writing them down, getting them out in the open, it will somehow help. Maybe contacting a reader or some spiritual person might help me be more loving than angry. I don't know.

I remember the day she died, finally getting back home. I started to scream. I don't remember all of what I said, but it was something like, "This is what I was afraid of all these years! This is what all the fights were about!"

I tried to keep her safe. I always felt that if I truly let go, everything would come apart. However, in her early twenties, I realized that I had to let go if we were going to have any relationship at all. So I let go as much as I could and watched her struggle and make mistakes, all the while holding my breath.

Then Brian came along. It was the best thing that ever happened to her. Brian was so good for her. We had so much fun planning the wedding. No fights like I'd heard about with other mothers and daughters. The three of us worked well together.

Courtney was still trying to fit into the work-a-day world and not doing too well. Again I felt as though I had accomplished something by just observing and not being judgmental. I guess I still feel that her life would have been easier if she'd had the inclination to study and work toward a degree in something to support herself and/or help Brian share the responsibility. She was living for the moment with short-term goals. I was feeling like I had failed in some way. Why couldn't Courtney be like everyone else?

I feel like I lost. Do I see everything as a contest—who's the best mother, best daughter? Whatever, I'm angry. I like to win. I like to have everything turn out my way. From the beginning, Courtney was not the way I had envisioned my daughter to be. So am I the first mother to be disappointed? Of course not! Even though on many levels we were like ships passing in the night, I miss her. I hope she didn't sense how disappointed I was—"angry" is the word—that she didn't finish college. Courtney was so hard for me to understand and to relate to. Ironically, she may have known her true course and was true to herself in spite of me. I guess she and I both thought we knew what was right. Ha! I don't know if any of this makes sense, but at least I got some of my feelings out.

November 24, 2001

We've had a wonderful time with our friends in Wheeling—just the four of us—for Thanksgiving dinner. I made it through after feeling weepy in the morning. John and I do have much to be thankful for: our health, our ability to do things like travel, our friends, our family, John's brother and his family, and my cousins. The list could go on and on.

I bought Christmas cards and gifts yesterday. I also bought an engagement plate made by Peggy Karr for Jason and Susan. It has an orange cat, a black-and-white cat, and sunflowers on it. I hope they like it. It's such a positive message being conveyed.

Last night we saw Marlo Thomas in *Paper Doll* in Pittsburgh. Pittsburgh is a wonderful city, and we ate at an Italian restaurant before the play. It was a comedy about Jacqueline Suzanne. Marlo did a great job—so did E. Murray Abraham. Suddenly I was remembering Marlo's book *Free to Be You and Me* that I'd read to Courtney. How we loved the stories! Then the tears started to come. I recovered quickly, so as not to cause anyone discomfort. I don't know why I feel this way or care, but I guess I don't want the attention and just want to be like everyone else.

December 25, 2001

It's Christmas—our second Christmas without Courtney. We're in Aiken, South Carolina, to meet our future daughter-in-law's family. In addition to her parents we also met her brother and sister-in-law, her maternal grandparents, and her sister.

Jason and Susan arrived in one piece from Russia, complete with

Luna, the cat. They are engaged! Susan loves her ring, which Jason had made especially for her. The Saturday before we left for Aiken, Jason and I drove to Granite to pick up the ring.

We are staying at Sandhurst Estate, a one-hundred-year-old mansion with high ceilings, wood floors, four-poster bed, marble bath, fireplace, and more. Aiken is a "horse" town, where the rich, northern industrialists summered as well as wintered.

Vacationing in a different place helps to ease the pain, or at least numb it. Nevertheless, Courtney is never far from us. It came back into focus when we talked to Brian today. He and Jen became engaged last night and are tentatively planning a November wedding, probably around Thanksgiving. I hope his family is as accepting of this as we are. We have to be. What other choice is there? We want him to be happy. We want him to consider himself part of our family, too. With the news of the engagement, I forgot to tell him that our godchild had a little girl. She named her Jade Courtney!

All-in-all we had a pleasant day. We have things to look forward to, but the pain is forever with us.

December 30, 2001

While we were in Aiken, I "saw" Courtney in a dream. We were in a theater and a mist or smoke kept drifting toward us. We left the area. It was then that I saw her. She had on a black scarf with black sunglasses, sort of the way Marilyn Monroe wore them. Courtney was standing and facing me but said not a word. She was just there.

January 1, 2002

A New Year's Prayer

To Whom It May Concern:
The Holy One, The Source, The Force, God, Goddess

Thank you for getting me through last year.

Thank you for all the gifts of friendship you've brought my way,

For my loving husband and son. May I be worthy of them.

Thank you for their safe travel to and from faraway places.

Thank you for giving me the opportunity to travel,

Bask in the climes of another country,

Feel the presence of the goddess where She was found in Austria,

Hear Mozart's Requiem and feel its power.

Thank you for giving me Brian and Susan.

May they always be a part of our family.

May I become more centered and organized,

with my priorities straight.

May my business continue to fund my life.

May I be an instrument to help my clients realize their dreams.

May I be a better listener.

When I speak, may I speak my truth.

January 4, 2002

A synopsis of December:

We attended thirteen events exclusive of Aiken and Mathews. We enjoyed all of them! At the Re/Max party, I danced to a rock-and-roll band. It felt good to dance. When I got to my car, I cried. That's an illustration of the ying and yang, the bitter and the sweet of last month. I never thought one could experience both at the same time.

January 21, 2002

Thirty years since Courtney was born! We bought roses to place at her tree and at Arlington. I had not seen the tombstone. The grief washed over me again. How exhausting but how necessary it is to give in to it. I talked with a friend about our individual grief. We're both distracted and forget things. It's like a "program" running in the background. We do our jobs, we start to pay attention to "It," and then we misplace something, forget, make a wrong turn, get mixed up.

After the ordeal of the cemetery, we found another Greek restaurant on East Capitol. Greek food always nurtures us. It still amazes me how grief grabs hold of us, squeezes the life out of us, then eases up, and we go forth to live another day!

UNSPEAKABLE!

We ran into a friend in Safeway's parking lot who had lost a son. He said he wished there was something he could say, but we all know there is nothing. His son's birthday is coming up soon.

We looked at slides from 1971 through 1979 tonight. It felt good to do that on Courtney's birthday. Some hard moments, but, all in all, it was a good idea.

Jason and Susan are almost back in Nahodka, Russia, where she will finish her Peace Corps obligation. They are supposed to call tonight. What a great time we had. We are thrilled that she will be part of our family. We have her cat, Luna, until they get back in October.

Brian sent an e-mail telling us that he and Jen are getting married at Fort Lewis on June 1. He wants to remain part of our family, and we want the same. We'll just do it somehow. He has to go on with his life. Whether he is making a mistake by moving too quickly, as his family thinks, only time will tell. Courtney was so lucky to have found and married Brian!

January 24, 2002

I have a stomach flu with dry heaves! A few tears come, but mostly today it was deep dry sobs. I wrote a long e-mail to Brian in response to his. I hope I made sense and didn't upset him.

I keep fluctuating between functioning with the awareness of my loss when I'm working and the awful, raw horror of the reality that she is gone. It doesn't seem real to me, but it's still somewhat comforting if indeed Anderson's book *Walking in the Garden of Souls* is true. I still have not been able to bring myself to call the psychic. Am I afraid? I don't think so. Am I reluctant to spend the money and be disappointed like I was last year with another psychic? I think that's a large part of it. The other part is that I'm not ready to hear from Courtney from the "other side." I want her *here* with me!

This living on without your child is such a painful, horrendous experience. Life will never be the same. George Anderson, in his book, says that bereaved parents are like empty shells trying desperately to fill themselves back up to be like their former selves. He also goes on to say that most parents are not afraid of dying, as the pain of the loss would then be gone.

I'm not ready to die, but I have thought of that. I know we will have happier times—such as Jason's wedding—but in the meantime, the pain is there. We don't want to forget her . The pain! Oh, the pain!

January 28, 2002

An elderly friend died yesterday after watching a football game with his kids. He got up and went to his bedroom to take a nap and never got up. That's the way to go.

A former youth minister spoke at church yesterday. She is now a Unitarian minister in Pennsylvania. She was the youth group leader when Courtney was in high school. Courtney loved her. I went up to her to let her know about Courtney's death. She had not heard. As I told her, the tears came along with the horror all over again. A friend stepped in and told her that Courtney's memorial was a wonderful service, and the church was packed with family and friends.

I don't know if it's because John is back in Russia (he just called!) or what. The grief I'm carrying is so heavy. I can almost feel it on my shoulders. The load seems lighter when John and I are together.

March 12, 2002

I'm fifty-seven! Had a pleasant weekend with dinners, calls, and cards from friends. Mike, my brother-in-law, sent a CD of pictures dating back to the seventies. I sure had two cute kids! An old friend called, and we talked forever. She got very emotional about not being at the memorial service. I guess we're all seeing the finite in everything by now.

In February I felt the weight of the burden I'm carrying. I got sick for the second time this year while in Sun Valley. These were the first illnesses I've had since Courtney died. It was good to be away, and I enjoyed the skiing I managed to do, but the way I felt brought me down. Our skiing friend called her daughter almost every day. I wish I could talk with Courtney again!

I saw a friend at a memorial service. She had not heard about Courtney's death. She said she does psychic readings and has started speaking with the dead.

I'm never sure about these "communications." The following are the main points "Courtney" made: She is with her baby in a state of bliss; she is waiting for me, but take my time; Nana was not there, but Pop is some kind of high priest or king in that family group of souls; Courtney visits John in dreams; Jason is very spiritual. He communicates with Courtney in dreams through "transmigration of souls." The most profound thing the reader said, and I did not understand it at first, was that Courtney saw her life as an "out of body" experience, especially her last year. After the session, it made more sense. Courtney had told me that all her life she would go "somewhere else" during her cardiac exams.

Over the weekend, we found the video she taped of the family reunion in Faribault, Minnesota, in 1996. To my disappointment, she was mostly behind the camera asking questions, making comments. I still want more of her intensity and personality to come through and to see her in videos. The weight lifted a little, and I was able to get through yet another birthday without her and her quirky birthday cards.

March 18, 2002

I dreamed of Courtney showing us a church or temple—some structure made of stone. There was a room inside, carpeted with comfortable furniture, like a lounge. Next, we were climbing the stairs with Brian. Again, I thought, *She's dead, but no one is commenting on it.* Courtney looked young, maybe twelve. Brian said, "Good-bye," and I said, "I didn't even get a chance to say hello." (That's what I'm afraid of now that he's getting married in two months.)

I also went to a healing service yesterday. When the priest laid his hands on my head, I could feel the energy. It was a meaningful service and one step along a very long path to where, I don't know. What does healing mean? That I don't cry every day? That I'm not constantly aware of a pain or ache in my heart? That I won't develop an illness from buried, unexamined feelings? That I'm healed because I've finished writing in this journal Courtney gave me?

April 1, 2002

Another Easter—this one not as raw as the last. I still can't buy into "hope" completely, but there is a glimmer.

UNSPEAKABLE!

The Queen Mum died Saturday; her daughter, Margaret, a month before. I guess she had had enough, and losing her daughter was too much. How many years of pain do I have left to endure?

April 10, 2002

Grief came back yet again with a vengeance, just as I thought it had lifted. I came home to find Brian's wedding invitation in the mail. Another "nail in the coffin," so to speak. All of my rationalizing and intellectualizing went right out the window. I want him to be happy, but I'm afraid that this will take him further away from us. Nothing will ever be the same.

May 9, 2002

These written comments, feelings, and perceptions are getting farther apart. I don't seem to have the need to write all the time. Also, I would be repeating myself. "Things are definitely not better. When will they be better? How could they?" Tomorrow I go back to Kripalu for a writing class, "Writing from the Heart." I need the break. Work is neither fun nor profitable this year.

It's Saturday morning. I'm sitting in class aware of my stomach. I don't know if it's the "salty" thing I picked for breakfast or if it's nerves or both. I'm going to hold myself open to what this experience has to offer me. There are "writers" in the group and others like me, who simply need to express themselves. My heart is breaking. I feel as though I'm falling into an abyss!

May 14, 2002

I don't want this journal Courtney gave me to be filled up, so I've stopped writing regularly. I was encouraged to write by the instructor of my writing class at Kripalu. This year it seemed there were so many mothers and daughters who came to take advantage of the many class offerings and experiences at Kripalu. If they were there last year, I blocked it.

I've titled the last page of this first journal, "Signs Along the Way."

- Courtney's last birthday card to Brian: "This is your year," and she wrote, "Miss me a little."

- Two adjacent oak trees in the backyard that held our hammock. One died and was cut down a few days before her death.

- Courtney told Brian that she was afraid of losing us. It concerned me, as I felt that for someone in her late twenties, she was too dependent on us.

- The fourth patio chair Courtney always sat in broke just before she died.

- Every time that last year when I was with her, something told me to give her a hug and kiss before she left.

- Before her death, Courtney contacted many people she hadn't talked to in a while.

UNSPEAKABLE!

May 22, 2002

Another "nail in the coffin": My emotions had been building up since Mother's Day. How many tears does one have to shed? Four to six years, so *they* say, before there is "transcendence." I don't understand what that means!

The incident that opened the flood gates: Brian called last week to thank me for the Peggy Karr platter I had given him and Jen for their wedding present. I reminded him that we had not gotten a picture of the wedding. Today he e-mailed it. I was at work and knew I shouldn't open it. I did anyway. The emotions were so strong that I had to leave work. It's a reality now. Jen isn't just a name connected with Brian; she's real. She's beautiful, and they make an attractive couple. Brian's remarriage has to be faced as well as meeting her sometime in the future.

I've been on a slippery slope since John left for Russia: Mother's Day, internet browsing to find more medical information on the average longevity of patients with Courtney's particular heart defect, and talking to Courtney's friend. It all adds up as if there were a ledger somewhere. There is no end, just muddling through.

June 11, 2002

I knew I was taking a chance going to the movie *Divine Secrets of the Ya-Ya Sisterhood*. I saw so many levels within the movie: my long time friends and me; Courtney and me; and the symbolism of the sunflower (the state flower of Kansas where she was born). Courtney would have liked the movie, too. She had read the book and even gave me the Ya-Ya calendar her last Christmas with us.

Movies, TV, and Theater

Courtney's love for movies, TV, and theater continued to grow as she got older. When she was around six, Star Wars *was popular. John and I saw the movie first and knew Courtney would love it. The unique characters fascinated her and stimulated her imagination. In upper elementary school, she used her persuasive powers on us to watch* Poltergeist *when they were first shown on TV. We reluctantly agreed, although we had our misgivings about allowing Courtney and Jason to watch it. After seeing* Poltergeist, *the kids went to bed. As we both predicted, Courtney and Jason came to our room with their sleeping bags. They were scared and couldn't go to sleep! John and I were not surprised and allowed them to curl up on our floor for the night.*

Courtney was prone to tape soap operas and movies. I remember she had taped Scream. *One night Jason and I decided to watch it. We were thoroughly involved when the movie stopped and another began. We sat with our mouths open! It could have been just a mistake or Courtney being Courtney!*

In middle school, the Molly Ringwald movies were popular. They provided a fun outing for Courtney and me. However, the most memorable movie she loved in early high school was The Breakfast Club. *Courtney watched it so many times, she knew almost all the dialogue! She identified with the characters because she had spent time in Saturday School herself. After this experience, I found a questionnaire (which she didn't return) that asked the students what had benefited them the most at Saturday School. One of the questions was "Do you think this experience will discourage you from returning to Saturday School?" Her answer: "It's totally my responsibility to complete my assignments." Courtney always sounded reasonable and sincere, but her words never matched her actions.*

As Courtney moved into her twenties, she would review and recommend movies for us to see. She particularly encouraged us to see Steel Magnolias, Terms of Endearment, *and* Ghost. *(She saw and recommended the movie* The Sixth Sense *the year she died.) When I saw these movies, I got an uneasy feeling. All of them were about a daughter dying! In retrospect, I feel it was a way for Courtney to communicate with us, through these movies, about her feelings and fear of her own death.*

Theater was another interest of hers. I had made it a point to take Courtney and Jason often. She was fascinated with Annie *as a little girl and delighted with* Cats *and* The Nutcracker Suite *in elementary and middle school. These performances also stimulated her imagination and encouraged her desire to be in plays and/or direct them. She got the chance to direct* Agnes of God *in high school. The play reflected her continued interest in the supernatural. It was Courtney's debut! We were so proud of her. She thought she and her cast had done a great job!*

All I have now is the past. The reality of only being able to talk about Courtney in the past tense is overwhelming. I can actually feel the heaviness and the pain. I see mothers and daughters, and it breaks my heart.

I dreamed of Courtney living here with us. She was with me doing various things. She went to the doctor and was told she shouldn't have a baby. She was upset. I heard it in her voice when she was telling me about it. I was looking out a window at the green grass and trees, and thinking that she probably would not be with us next year and to simply enjoy her now, in the present.

Last weekend we went to Kansas City to see our goddaughter's baby, Jade Courtney, for the first time. What a cutie, and so person-able already! The weekend was bittersweet, as most experiences seem to be. We talked a lot about Courtney. Again, we speak always in the past tense. Of course that's all we can do now. It was hard to see them going on with their life in its natural progression while we're frozen in time.

July 3, 2002

I somehow feel a comfort this morning. Happy sixty-ninth anniver-sary, Mom and Pop! Happy birthday to you, Uncle Estell! Although they have passed, I still remember the dates.

July 12, 2002

It's been forty-two years since Grandma Curry died. I still miss her. It's the same with my parents, aunts, and uncles. It's the feeling of the absence of their support and knowledge; of family, acceptance, and love. And yet I do feel it when I think of them all or see the family movies. I feel them again, but it is still upsetting because they aren't physically here. I guess it is longing for the stability and protection that I once had and have no longer.

I haven't been able to get information on the Internet of the life expectancy of children with "Transposition of the Great Vessels."

UNSPEAKABLE!

One of Courtney's friends has started working at Johns Hopkins Hospital. She checked in the library and found that their life expectancy is to their mid-twenties. I guess we weren't going to have her long no matter what. I have to believe she was serious about "The Lady" or angel. Courtney talked about her so consistently. I wonder if, as one gets close to death, one starts to "see them." Pop and an elderly friend saw entities. There is so much I want to talk about with Courtney!

July17, 2002

I went to DC to get a visa for our trip to China. I stopped at Arlington cemetery first and took some flowers to Courtney's grave. This may be obvious to anyone else, but I've always gotten upset at the cemetery.

Imagine you're dreaming, walking in a cemetery full of tombstones of people you don't know. Suddenly, you see a stone with your child's name on it. That sounds and feels like a nightmare, only I live it every time I go there. Today was particularly surreal. I guess it's not so bad when John or someone else is with me. The shock of seeing her stone is still there, to a greater or lesser degree. The dogwood, on the other hand, although her ashes are buried with the roots, is a living thing. I never realized the difference until today! Grief takes a lot out of me. It's also hot, hot, hot! I'm exhausted!

August 2, 2002

I dreamed that we were someplace I didn't recognize. Brian was there, and so was Courtney. I took a picture of them kissing and holding each other. Then I saw Courtney in a swing in the backyard. She looked thinner and younger, and her hair was short. Brian was pushing her in the swing. In both of these parts of the dream, they were no longer married but still had feelings for one another. I did think that Courtney did not look or act upset that Brian was with someone else now. She was just enjoying the moment.

August 28, 2002

It's been two years and a day. John and I took off work yesterday to spend the day together. We went to the cemetery and put purple roses on her grave. Brian had told us several years ago that she liked purple or lavender roses. In fact, according to a "new age" friend, Courtney "came through" and told our friend to give us four lavender roses and a yellow rose. The five represent the circle of life. They are beautiful!

How do I feel? I'm numb. I'm exhausted. I'm discouraged. I don't feel any letup. I don't see any transcendence. I'm just getting through the day, and according to Buddha, that's just the way it is. I don't seem to have anything extra to give.

September 3, 2002

One of our longtime friends and the mother of one of John's best friends died yesterday. What a blessing! It's a mystery to me why she lasted as long as she did. People with Alzheimer's tend to outlive their spouses, as was the case with her husband, who died first. I realized only after Courtney died that they unknowingly became a role model for us after their son, Johnny, died in Vietnam. When we would visit them, we could feel his presence as we looked at the many pictures of him around their house. I hope she is with her husband and son once again.

The pall has lifted somewhat. We're getting ready for our trip to China.

September 14, 2002

I have been so busy seeing the sights here in Beijing that I haven't had time to write. We had dinner with friends from Columbia who live here now. Their work has brought them to Beijing. We were served vegetarian food and an Egyptian/Chinese mix. Susie, their daughter, and her Egyptian in-laws (who are Bahai's) were there. They told us that they would be killed for leaving Islam if they returned to Egypt.

Apparently Susie did not know or had forgotten that Courtney had died. They had been friends in our congregation's youth group. It was quite a shock to her, and of course she wanted to know the particulars. It was very hard for me, but I got through it. To see shock and horror register on another's face brings back into focus how horrible and devastating this experience was and is and will continue to be. We're learning to live with the absence of Courtney. The edge of the knife in our hearts has dulled, but the point is still sharp. (Surprisingly, there are no further references to Courtney in the journal I kept on the trip.)

November 13, 2002

It's been a while since I've written anything. There has been a "shift" of some sort since I got back from China. Having Jason and Susan here has helped. They are such fun and have such good energy. The cats, Garfield and Luna, are happy, too.

I had a "reading" October 21. I haven't processed it all yet. I think that has contributed to the shift, whether it was a hoax or not. The shift appears to be a resignation, almost an acceptance of Courtney's death. She is with me but on the periphery, as if she is just "away," as Jason was while in Russia. It comes into focus now and then but not as intense or for any length of time.

As an example, I was watching an interview with Robin Williams. I was laughing until they showed a clip of Robin in Afghanistan with the soldiers. I started crying as I realized that many of those young soldiers would die, as John's friend and Courtney had. It took a while to stop.

Two nights ago I was dozing on the couch. Someone was kissing me on the cheek. It looked like Courtney, or it felt like her. When I opened my eyes, I could still feel where she kissed me. I think that was the first time I've been aware of her. I'm letting myself feel her presence, whether it's pretending or not. It makes me feel better.

December 27, 2002

It's our thirty-seventh anniversary! Wow! It doesn't seem that long ago. However, lots of events have happened in our lives: good, bad, wonderful, exciting, disappointing, and scary. All in all, it's been a good life together, and it looks as though it will continue to be.

UNSPEAKABLE!

This was our first Christmas at home since Courtney died. Jason and Susan were with us, which made it more bearable. Susan is such a joy. She's a person who finds humor in the littlest things. Jason and John even rose to the occasion and had fun!

I think the thing that made it work this Christmas was all of the planning we did for the day. After much debate, we decided to cut down a Christmas tree. Of all the activities the past two weeks, the tree—choosing it, cutting it down, and decorating it—was the hardest. Hanging Courtney's stocking was the worst!

Christmas Eve was special, although John didn't go to church with us. He felt it would be too upsetting with the Christmas music and everyone there with their kids. After singing we came back home for champagne and mussels. Each of the four of us read something: Jason, *Giving* by Khalil Gibran; Susan, *The Night Before Christmas*; John from the Tao; and me, "Christmas Day" from *The Little House in the Big Woods*.

The most beautiful thing that happened was the unexpected snow! It made the holiday special. And it did not stop nor prevent our friends from joining us for Christmas dinner. Throughout this difficult season, Susan kept us in the present, enjoying the moment, which is, after all, the only thing we have!

January 19, 2003

(You will begin to notice the journal entries becoming farther apart. During these breaks, the need to write diminished as my focus was on work, my family, travel, etc. I wasn't driven to write as often. At the same time, my grief and pain became the "norm," my reality and constant companion.

Also from this year on, almost every other entry is written in the style of a poem. I hadn't expressed myself in this way before. The poems flowed from me naturally. Instead of writing in prose to describe my feelings, I was often compelled to write in this form.)

Reflection at the Cemetery

How did it come to this?

My shadow on her tombstone.

Her name inscribed with her birth and death.

How did we come to this?

A blustery January day much like long ago

when there was anticipation and hope:

snow falling, wind blowing.

How did we come to this?

Two middle-aged souls with nowhere to go.

Our stewardship over, our caring for her over.

No worries now. No concern for her welfare

or what she should be doing. Free...

UNSPEAKABLE!

How did we come to this?

We follow a car along the lanes of Arlington National Cemetery.

"Oh God, no!"

A car slowly makes its way past the white stones,

paying respect to the soldiers and family members

who once lived.

The car's license plate: "1son911."

Those of us who have lost a child have to bear the unbearable,

the unspeakable,

the unimaginable!

We have come to make our pilgrimage to a cold stone

on a cold January day.

How did we come to this?

By hope, by faith, by determination that her life

would be nurtured as long as was needed.

By denial that the worst case would ever happen.

We are here, as so many other parents, paying tribute:

To affirm her existence, to lay the flowers,

To speak her name yet once again to all those who will listen,

To remember the fun times,

the incidental and everyday occurrences.

We leave the stone, a testimony that she lived.

January 29, 2003

This is an exercise to keep away the demons of self-doubt. Thich Nhat Hanh, in his book *No Death, No Fear*, recommends that we try to stay in the moment and be in our natural state, which is happiness. It's a tall order!

My business is capricious at best. I've had four listing appointments this month: two with competing agents and two with people who want me to represent them. I guess 50 percent isn't bad. So I wait to get the news, second-guessing and "Monday morning quarterbacking". I ask myself whether this will make a difference in my year. Perhaps. It didn't last year. Will it make a difference five to ten years from now? No.

My positive accomplishments today: meditation, exercise, prepared for tonight's listing presentation, wrote a blurb for *Business Women's Network*, made a good dinner, and ended the day with my cat, Luna, lying snugly next to me in bed.

February 28, 2003

I got up and realized that I don't cry every morning as I used to. It's been thirty months yesterday since Courtney died. I had lunch with a friend, who lost her husband to cancer on February 3. She is in shock and disbelief, and I hope I was a distraction for her, at least for a little while. I later talked to another friend who had lost her son the year after Courtney died. We talked about how hard it still was but we were "moving on". I hate that term! I prefer "muddling through."

Yesterday, I turned on the *Today Show* and learned that Mr. Rogers had died. It brought back memories of that time in our lives. It was all over. It wasn't that I was horribly sad about his death; he had lived a wonderful life and contributed so much to children. It was the memories of a little curly headed girl, all bright eyed and full of curiosity and creativity, that came back to me. Courtney loved the puppets. She loved how Mr. Rogers talked in that slow, patient voice.

I went on the Fred Rogers website and unexpectedly found his episode about death. He encouraged parents to listen to their children when they talk about dying. One little boy said he didn't want to grow up because he would die and be separated from his parents.

That again reminded me of what Brian told us: Courtney had said she had a tremendous fear of losing us. When I later mentioned this to her, she wouldn't comment on it. I doggedly went on talking about how it was a natural occurrence for parents to die before their children. In retrospect, I feel what she was upset about was her losing us by *her* dying.

For the rest of the day I was back to square one. All those days are gone. I have to focus, enjoy, and look forward to what I have now and will have in the future. To do otherwise will sap my energy. The feelings and memories are still there. They will never go away entirely.

Today is a new day. We have more snow! I will enjoy this day, as it's the only one I have.

March 11, 2003

(Every birthday, anniversary, wedding, or funeral, the loss comes back into focus.)

I'm fifty-eight today. How can that be? Why am I still here, for what? (John just called me as he was walking to work to wish me a happy birthday.) As mundane as we think life is, that's precisely why we are here! I think of Courtney. She only had twenty-eight birthdays. I've lived thirty years longer than she was given. And yet she was given those twenty-eight years that could have been denied to her at birth. Can't that be said for all of us?

So today I'm grateful. I'm grateful for my health, my abilities, my family, my friends, and my experiences. My only regret is that Courtney is not here. There is still the ache of missing her, of not always being there for her, of guilt for what I should have done. At the bottom of it all, I know I/we did the best we could, and she knew it, too. Why am I given the years? I get to see the babies of her friends and wonder what her baby would have been like. Why are we deprived of this joy? The longer you live, the more questions and fewer answers you have!

April 28, 2003

(I wrote the following poem a month before Jason's wedding.)

Bitter and Sweet

Spring is here.

Life has been renewed.

The daffodils we planted came up from a sound sleep

to brighten our days.

Your dad is playing softball again with the other "old geezers"!

The world has turned once again.

The seasons continue to come and go.

Life ebbs and flows.

You are not with us.

A celebration is on the horizon.

Most of the plans are in place.

ANGER!

The excitement is mounting,

Recalling another time.

Remember?

Much thought has gone into the ceremony, the clothes,

the flowers, the music. Remember?

It's Jason's turn.

Where are you?

There won't be a special place for you with the bridesmaids.

There won't be a funny story told by "Sister."

No special blessing given by you.

Oh! The void you've made!

The space left unfilled!

The proud sister not seen!

Yes, we will talk, laugh, and dance, celebrating

this milestone in your brother's life.

We will share the happiness for a little while.

It will be bittersweet nevertheless.

You are not here.

May 27, 2003

After all the activity and excitement of the wedding, I dreamed of Courtney. I was at a picnic table filling out a form. I got to the middle and realized that I had written "Courtney Baker" and not Slosman. Courtney, in her usual off-hand manner, said that it was OK to do that, as she didn't use Slosman anymore. She was "back." I wondered if it was because she had gotten out of the marriage by feigning her death so Brian would go on to the army and find someone new. Her hair was that dark brownish-red. She was not looking at me directly, as she was prone to do when she was doing something I questioned. She was nonchalantly drinking a soda. There was no baby with her.

June 11, 2003

The Storm

It's raining again, lightning and thunder, as it did the

night you died.

How did we get home?

We could hardly see!

The defroster didn't work.

Shock!

How did we make it home?

We thought it was just another trip to the emergency room.

We joked that we were going to see

what Northwest's emergency room was like.

Or was that just me and my denial talking?

Your father knew all along.

I didn't get it.

Not when the receptionist said wait a minute.

Not when the security guard came to get us.

Not when he wasn't making small talk.

Not when he took us to a small room filled

with your ambulance friends and a cop.

Not when the doctor and nurse entered the room.

UNSPEAKABLE!

Only when she calmly said, "Courtney has died."

As if she were casually saying,

"Courtney has been born,"

"Courtney has graduated,"

"Courtney is married."

Only then did I get it.

I got it in spades.

I got it delivered as one of those lightning bolts outside.

I had been fearing those words since you were born.

Disorientation!

Shock!

Pain!

Upset stomach.

Your father pacing, holding his hand to his chest,

and saying, "It hurts, it hurts!"

You left us! We didn't leave you! We never would have left you!

ANGER!

Only in old age.

When our time was up.

It was natural.

It was done, our journey together.

At last I was through with hospitals!

Twenty-eight years along hospital corridors,

in doctors' offices, EKGs, ECKOs,

cardiac caths.

Just fix it so we can forget about it and live a "normal" life!

There was no "fixing" anymore.

I remember saying to Jason just a few weeks before

"We can't fix her."

"Courtney is responsible for her own life."

Yet as I write this, anger at you for not being responsible

starts bubbling up.

How could you inflict so much pain on us?

How could you let us go?

UNSPEAKABLE!

Everything go?

I'm spent.

I've emptied myself, at least for now, until the next time.

Is there no end to grief?

It ebbs and flows.

Mr. Luna is on the end of the bed.

I sometimes think when I look at cats, I'm close to you.

Whether it is true or not, it makes me smile, most of the time.

My kitten is gone.

I only see your reflection.

Cats

Cats became a constant presence in our family from the time Courtney was four. Her dad and I did not particularly like cats because of unpleasant experiences with them when we were children. She had a lifelong affinity for the care and love of animals, but especially cats, which persisted all her life.

One day Courtney came home from nursery school and told us her teacher's cat had a litter of kittens. She needed to find homes for them. Courtney asked if she could have one of the kittens. We told her we'd think about it. She was very persistent, and we finally consented. This was just the beginning of using her powers of persuasion by making what she wanted to do seem logical and a "good" idea!

The kitten came to live with us in 1976. She was gray, black, and white. It was the year of the bicentennial, so we called her Abigail after Abigail Adams. Courtney was great with her and helped with her feeding. Abigail was a one-person cat, and that person was Courtney—especially when her two-year-old brother, Jason, pestered her! John and I were merely tolerated.

One day Abigail was grazed by a car. We did not see her for several days. Courtney was very upset and thought she was dead. We told her that sometimes cats will disappear after a traumatic event to lick their wounds and get themselves back together. Eventually she returned, and surprisingly all was well. That was the first of Abigail's nine lives.

Abigail flew with us to visit my parents in Florida before we moved from Maryland to California in 1979. I let her out, as she was an indoor/outdoor cat, assuming she would not run off. One night she did not come home when I called her. When she finally came to the door, she was bleeding. She must have tangled with an armadillo or something. We took her to the vet, who told us she would be fine with some medication. Of course that became my job. Inserting an antibiotic into a cat's wounds is not fun. That was two lives. Abigail had seven more to go!

Abigail survived the plane ride to San Jose and settled in right away. One day Courtney came home with a black kitty she found on the

UNSPEAKABLE!

Paseo near our house. Again she begged us to keep her. What's another cat? She named the cat, Kizzy, after the character in Roots. Abigail didn't seem to mind the newcomer, and the two got along well.

In 1979, cats were dying of feline leukemia before the vaccine was available. Kizzy was the first to die, followed by Abigail a few months later. It was all very sad. Courtney and Jason had a funeral for each of them. We buried them in the backyard under our lemon trees.

Another kitten, Elliott, died shortly after we got him. After that, we went a couple of years without any animals except for an ant farm and fish. By 1984 Courtney was twelve. She and Jason had been asking for a dog and a cat for a while. I wasn't particularly keen on it, as I had heard of mothers ending up responsible for the total care and feeding, not to mention walking the dog! We had many long conversations about the responsibility they would need to take on. Of course they both said they would care for them, but I wanted to be at least 80 percent sure they meant it. I told them that before we got the pets, they would have to sign an agreement stating that the care and feeding was their responsibility. (I have never heard of any other parent do this!) I wrote a short agreement and they signed it. To my surprise, both Courtney and Jason complied with it. The care of their pets was never an issue.

A short time later, I saw an ad in the paper for two kittens who needed a home. By this time we had agreed to two cats and a dog. (Courtney's and now Jason's powers of persuasion were limitless!) The kids and I drove over to the address where the kittens were living at the time. There was a black-and-white female and an orange male tabby. They were found on the doorstep of the man who was trying to find a home for them. He lived next to the Almaden Hills and thought they had come from a feral litter.

The kittens were just what we were looking for! We named the black-and-white female Buttons and the male, Garfield. What a pair! Lots of antics to the delight of all of us—well, maybe not John! It was fun to watch them arching their backs in front of the mirror in our bedroom, preparing to meet an enemy. John didn't think it was so funny when they pulled the table cloth off the dining room table, rolling around under it and having a great time!

A couple of months later, we got Maxwell, a Cairn Terrier. Again both children took care of all three of them. However, Courtney was still primarily a "cat person," so Jason took over the responsibility of taking the dog to obedience training (that's Jason's story!) and walking him twice a day.

Courtney then asked if we would let Buttons have kittens. I thought it would be a good experience for the children, so I consented. Their dad was outnumbered and washed his hands of the whole thing!

Soon tomcats were in our yard yowling for more days than I care to remember. After that, Buttons was "with kittens." Courtney and Jason were thrilled, and we looked forward to their birth. It was incredible to see Maxwell and Garfield defer to Buttons when they ate, drank, and went outside.

One day, as the time approached for the kittens to be born, Buttons started to prepare a "nest" in Courtney's cluttered closet. We put down old sheets and newspapers. Soon six beautiful kittens were born.

Buttons was a very good mother. A few days later I got the bright idea to move the kittens downstairs so we could keep an eye on them. She would have none of it! Buttons returned all of them, one at a time, back upstairs to Courtney's closet.

UNSPEAKABLE!

Meanwhile Garfield and Maxwell were very interested in the new kittens. We kept an eye on the two of them, as we didn't know how they would behave. One day I came home while the kids were still at school. I went upstairs to see how the kittens were doing. Buttons only had three in her nest! Where were the other three? Then I heard lapping and licking sounds from under the bed. I froze! Garfield and Maxwell are eating the kittens! What was I going to do? I had to do something before the children got home and saw the carnage. I stood there for a few minutes before I got up enough courage to look under the bed. I shouldn't have worried. All was well. The absent kittens were getting a bath from their uncles! What a surprise and a relief! I related what happened to Courtney and Jason when they got home. They were astounded. It has been a favorite family story ever since.

As I was writing about Courtney's love of cats, I realized we wouldn't have had these experiences, as well as many others, without Courtney's powers of persuasion!

Courtney the Day Before Surgery March – 1973

Courtney and Infant Jason – 1975

Courtney and Hand Puppet Production – 1979

Courtney & Jason – 1980

Courtney as Costume Designer – 1982

Courtney with Abigail – 1983

Courtney Director of Agnes of God – 1991

Courtney & Kay – 1992

Courtney's Wedding – 1997

Courtney and Her Family at the Grand Tetons – 1999

CHAPTER 3

On the Outside Looking In

August 27, 2003

It's been three years since Courtney died.

Another Anniversary

Losing a child means never, never mending the wound,

filling the void, the abyss.

That child who was your dream, your hope, your challenge, your pride.

Today we are voyeurs.

We watch from the outside as children grow, graduate, marry,

and have children.

UNSPEAKABLE!

We are the walking wounded.

We are told, "You've done so well."

Getting out of bed and going to work is what they are talking about.

There is no other choice for us!

We have to partake in life as it comes.

Weddings and celebrations.

Our son, our nieces and nephews, our friends, Courtney's friends.

They are left with an emptiness in their hearts, too.

We need to enjoy the gifts that are given to us.

We cannot have her back.

We can, however, be reminded of her when we see

Cats,

Movies,

The moon and stars,

Pagan holidays,

Halloween,

Angels and fairies.

August 28, 2003

It happened. The dam finally broke. All of my coping mechanisms failed. It feels as though my heart has split open. We tried to act "normal" when we met Jen. I hope it worked. It was tough making conversation, but we did it. Maybe the next time we see her it won't be as difficult. Other parents have done it; so can we. Jen appeared to be nervous around us at the family gatherings. It must have been awkward for her to make small talk.

They weren't here long. Brian came to get Courtney's china and crystal. Maybe he and Jen will use them. I remember Courtney fixing dinner on those plates. She enjoyed using them. I'm sure Courtney would have wanted Brian and Jen to have them, as material things weren't that important to her. To me it felt as though they were taking her hopes and dreams.

After they left, I lost it. I had been holding it together the last few days. The emotions of the past three years ripped open my heart yet again. Now I know what "keening" means and what it feels like. John said I sounded like a banshee! It scared him. There was no "stiff upper lip" or "taking it on the chin." I felt as if I didn't have the energy to maintain my public face anymore. John held me until I calmed down. Garfield was close by, purring. That cat!

I'm scared after this episode. I've taken several steps backward. I'm afraid of my rage. How many tears must I shed? I don't think I'll ever be back to "normal," whatever that means. I can't bear to think of the many things that were denied Courtney and us. It's the unfairness of it all.

September 8, 2003

(The following poem expressed my frustration over my grief, which continued with the same feelings over and over again, with seemingly no let up.)

Time Means Nothing

Three years! I'm still writing about your death.

I wrote about it on the twenty-seventh.

I didn't remember it until now!

Still I write.

Haven't I cried enough?

Haven't I missed you enough?

No, there is always more.

Is there no end?

Your dad and I are alone with your loss, our loss.

Everyone else has gone on with their lives.

There is hole, this void you left.

You filled our lives for so long.

It's a big hole to fill.

Now it's empty. What do we do?

Where do we go?

You kept us busy.

You kept us involved, whether we wanted to be or not!

Three years of emptiness without you.

Three years going through the motions.

Three years.

December 15, 2003

A Party

There was a Christmas party at work.

Nice restaurant.

Plenty of food.

Lots to drink; for some, too much.

Good music to dance to.

Everyone smiling, dancing, enjoying themselves.

Some, a smile painted on their faces.

UNSPEAKABLE!

What is behind the posturing, the pretty clothes?

Honest people who have worked hard for years,

The gears in the wheels of the economy.

They make people's dreams come true.

I watch.

I make small talk.

I dance.

I have a drink, smile, and laugh.

This year feels as though I'm going through the motions.

(Hasn't it been this way for three years?)

Now I'm awake and aware.

I've awakened from a bad dream.

I see things now for what they really are.

I really am on the outside looking in, watching people live their lives.

They've forgotten.

I haven't.

ON THE OUTSIDE LOOKING IN

This is a time of hope—for some.

This is a time of joy—for some.

This is a time to get through as best I can.

What is the lesson from this dark time of year?

I wish I knew.

I get no joy from the cards lauding how good

God has been to them this year.

How he has "blessed" them and their family.

If that were true and I haven't been blessed,

I couldn't bear to live another day.

What is this materialistic, pseudo-religious,

forced sociability all about?

It's about gathering together,

Wishing each other well,

Giving each other courage to keep on keeping on.

It is about hope, hope that the sun will come back to warm the earth.

UNSPEAKABLE!

The fires, the gathering of friends and family

will protect us from the darkness,

The unknown—even death.

December 31, 2003

I had a "good" year. Let me count the good things.

1. Business was the best.

2. Having fun in the snow in our backyard with three twenty year olds!

3. Jason and Susan got married.

4. Helping them with the wedding to-do list.

5. Hosting the rehearsal dinner in the Inner Harbor.

6. A crab feast the day after!

7. Sailing in the British Virgin Islands.

8. Dancing in a limbo contest on the isle of Anegada and coming in third!

9. Seeing many of my old friends at my fortieth high school reunion.

10. Meeting an old woman at the cemetery where my

parents are buried who had known my dad and mother. She remembered they had a pretty, curly headed little girl. Moi!

11. Seeing my one-hundred-year-old English teacher was awe-inspiring.

12. Talking to old friends.

13. A boat ride on the St. Croix River.

14. Fireworks on the DC mall.

15. Remodeling our kitchen and baths.

16. Christmas with Aunt Marian and my cousins in Seattle.

February 27, 2004

I dreamed that John and I were sitting with a group of people talking. Courtney was there, too. She was talking and being her old self as we knew her. I think she got up to leave, and someone commented about her. I said she was like that in life, but what they saw was an "illusion." She had died. (I think that's what I said, instead of "she is a ghost.") No one, including myself, was afraid or upset. I was merely stating a fact.

February 28, 2004

It never ceases to amaze me how one can be dropped from a tall

UNSPEAKABLE!

building at the most unexpected moments!

We were invited to the wedding of one of Jason's friends. What an occasion to see this young man grown up! The setting was a castle at Marydale School. The ceremony was short. My feet were hurting from standing in heels as we watched everyone dance. We got a piece of the wedding cake. It was then that "It" happened. We were watching the bride dance with her father when the memory of Courtney's wedding came back into focus.

Oh, the horror! We've learned to live with our loss until it rises to the surface once more. In that instant we become watchers, observers—those on the outside looking in. Then the pain starts seeping out of our pores. The sense of the unfairness. Why our daughter? We're back to square one once more.

June 5, 2004

(Many times I would worry about getting sick with a terminal disease. I couldn't imagine why I hadn't gotten something with all the stress. After writing in my journal, I was able to refocus and go on with my day.)

I can't believe it's been three months since I've written in this journal!

Jason and Susan left on March 31 and are settled in Baku, Azerbaijan. It will be such an adventure for them! It's been harder for John and me than we thought. Now I know how my parents felt when I left home. Paybacks are tough. We are left to redefine ourselves. After a year of activity, excitement, and laughter, it has been taken away. It seems as though the presence of Jason and Susan softened living without Courtney. It lightened the load. Now it's back with a vengeance. No, not "gone." It lifts. I feel lighter. I can cope.

I have to go back and get a "compression" mammogram. Evidently they saw something they didn't like in my right breast! Am I surprised? Yes and no. Do I think it's cancer? Maybe. My rational mind says "no." My irrational mind says, "Oh no!" I guess I've been waiting for the "other shoe to drop." After the shock John and I have had, I've been waiting for some kind of health problem to pop up. I feel nothing unusual when I do my self-exam. Both breasts seem the same. I'm making myself sick before I have something to be sick about. When I do this, it wastes my time and energy. Nonetheless, I'm awake at 2:00 a.m.!

As we get closer to June 16, when we leave for our niece's wedding, things are looking up and accelerating as usual: business better, mood a little better, anxiety still there.

That's what's going on June 5. Tune in next week...

June 14, 2004

Two days before we leave for Hawaii! It will be great to get away for a few days—seventeen, to be exact!

August 1, 2004

(Our twenty-year-old cat, Garfield, died at the end of July.)

121

UNSPEAKABLE!

Garfield!

Twenty years you were our companion, our sentinel, our constant!

What a will you had!

What fortitude!

How will life be without you?

We bonded immediately.

We connected again after Courtney left home.

You calmed me with your purrs, your body lying on mine.

You were a constant joy and delight.

The memories:

You and Buttons tangled in the tablecloth!

Helping Buttons with her kittens. What a great uncle!

You were the one who let me know when Buttons was hit by a car.

How proud you were when you caught the bunny -

until Courtney screamed!

No more trophies for us to see!

ON THE OUTSIDE LOOKING IN

Your quiet presence through these past four years

since Courtney died.

Your not-so-quiet presence when you wanted us

to get up and feed you.

You had a slick routine

meowing,

cold nose,

head butting.

teeth gently on my head!

Your spirit would not give up,

even though your body could not continue.

We'll miss you, Garfield!

There will never be a cat quite like you!

Your spirit will remain in our hearts forever.

August 6, 2004

A Blessing for Parents

Blessings to those who have lost children,

it is unnatural,

out of order,

out of sync.

Blessings to those who have lost grandchildren.

To lose a child, or grandchild, is to lose your

Hope,

Your dreams,

Your optimism,

Your joy,

Your wonder,

Your belief in magic.

Blessings to those who carry this weight.

May it become lighter but not forgotten.

August 19, 2004

Swans

Their cygnet, their baby, died!

How? Why? I don't know.

They had two in the spring.

One died.

One lived.

How they cared for him!

The three swimming, gliding over the lake!

Now it too is gone!

The parents left to glide alone.

The two of them, as before.

September 20, 2004

I need to make lists of positives in my life! Life has come crashing in again, sending me back to square one!

- Business is good

- I painted Jason's old room.

- The hardwood floors have been refinished as well as the dining room set.

- We've had barbecues with friends.

- I took my turn as a worship associate.

- I've given blood two or three times this year.

- I enjoyed Hawaii: rainbows, fish, birds, beaches, and family.

- I bought the Lexus that was on my to-do list!

- I enjoyed solitude in my backyard. (What's happened to the "party girl"?)

- I take comfort in old friends.

September 21, 2004

I'm still having trouble sleeping. I'm anxious over media stories of death. I'm avoiding people so I don't have to answer questions. I'm still watching other's lives go by—weddings, grandchildren. I'm questioning why all this has happened and what role I played in it. I feel lack of control and panic!

(Often I would find myself going over and over again the "what-ifs." It really does no good. My therapist recommended that I write a letter to Courtney as an exercise to express my anger to her.)

Dear Courtney,

It's been four years since you left us. I still can't believe those words: "Courtney has died." Twenty-eight years. In my mind you are frozen in time, and we are the ones who continue to live and breathe and grow old. You didn't have that luxury. You were denied the further trials, tribulations, joys, and anticipation of this life.

I recently ordered Linda's wedding gift. Do you remember your joint birthday parties? She is getting married October 24. She picked out a beautiful Royal Doulton pattern. So did you once. Once you had hope and anticipation of life with Brian. I'm happy for Linda, but I'm angry that you were denied life so soon.

I guess I'm angry about a lot of things concerning your death. You should have been thinking! *Why didn't you go to the hospital? It never stopped you before! That is all water under the bridge. You're dead! We can't go back and rewrite your story. We—and you—can't change anything. It truly was a bad soap opera with a bad ending.*

I have not spent too much time feeling guilty. However, I have wondered whether the outcome would have been different if you had simply come to our house that day as planned. We should have insisted you live with us while Brian was in Georgia. I truly don't think you and I would have done anything different. We were both trying to separate from one another: you, becoming more independent as an adult; me, trying to keep my mouth shut!

Oh, I still worried about you, and I had things I thought you needed to hear, but when you were over at our house, I couldn't "remember" what it was I needed to talk to you about! We probably would have fought anyway. I'm glad I didn't have that talk with you! I'm also glad that I listened to that "small voice" and gave you a hug and a kiss every time you left.

I can remember our last meal together: crabs. I can't pick crabs any-more. I think it was the day you told me "The Lady" had moved to your house. You thought she was your guardian angel. I felt relief! Everything would be fine!

You've left us holding the bag of grief. There are still so many questions.

You've left us! We have no hope. You were our hope. Our miracle baby! Our survivor! We live with despair and rage. I see your peers with babies—three-year-olds. It's getting worse. Time does not heal. It only makes it clear that this void continues to grow—there's no filling it. There's no place for it! I, we, all three of us have to learn to live without you. Why should we? Why us? Why you?

I never felt I was up to the task of being your mother. We certainly butted heads a lot. You had your agenda. I had mine. I still find myself wondering whether, if I had done this or that, it would have made a difference. We both know the answer to that. We were both strong-willed, so there was bound to be conflict. I did blame myself when things weren't going right in your life. So I have purposely not played the "blame game" since you've died. Our relationship was what it was. It was a work in progress. Now it's done, and that hurts. The pain is unimaginable!

Garfield died in July. He was our sentinel, our comforter. Every change or perceived change magnifies or brings into focus your loss and compounds it. They are separate things—they are the same— in terms of feelings.

When you died, I thought nothing could hurt me ever again. The challenge was learning to live without you. Now, four years later, nothing has changed: tears are always near the surface; every death brings it into focus again. I'm doing all the right things: exercise, yoga, meditation. I call your name when I light a candle. We planted a tree along with some of your ashes. The bottom line is that we miss you: all your quirkiness, stubbornness, messiness, your movie reviews, books, etc. There's no replacing you! It's so final. There's no getting over it! There's no sense of it being easier as time goes by. Your dying came before mine; that's backwards. You're in my thoughts daily. When I remember events, it's either before you died or after.

If you need us to let you go so your soul, as some people believe, can go on, I'm afraid we can't do that. I thought so for a while—until this year. Now I don't know. That will be your problem! Oh, I wish we could communicate! Maybe that would help. Sometimes I feel you around me.

Blessings to you, even though I'm angry.

Blessings to you for all you gave us.

Blessings to you for all you taught us.

Blessings to you for your courage throughout your life!

Love,

Mom

October 13, 2004

I woke at 3:00 a.m. I felt panic watching life and not being able to do anything about it. I'm constantly worrying about what is coming next. Intellectually, I know that nothing is permanent. I want predictability, yet there is none. I want to laugh again and have things to look forward to.

My sister-in-law's mother died Monday. She leaves a huge family who will miss her. She leaves good memories. She didn't want to miss a thing. What will I leave?

There are three of us now all trying to find our place in the world. What does the future hold? What did I do wrong to arrive here? Everything seems to be unraveling! Why am I here at this place in time? How are we going to fill our lives from now on and with whom? I feel more in control when I'm working—yet I don't always have control there either. I feel more in control when I'm doing something—anything to focus on besides how empty life seems now. What do I want in the future for me—for the three of us?

(Another list. I continued to find this so helpful as some days it was the best thing for me to do.)

My goals for our family:

- Strengthen my role as wife and mother

- Communicate our love for each other

- Doing fun things together

- Travel

- Buy a condo

- Something, anything, that all of us can focus on

October 29, 2004

My cousin called with bad news. Her brother was killed in a construction accident! Everyone is with my aunt, stunned, shocked, dismayed. Another nightmare!

Wake me up. Is there no end to this? I'm stuck at the beginning with shock and disbelief all over again.

November 9, 2004

My therapist recommended making the following list of things I would have done differently in raising Courtney:

I would have realized early on that Courtney was not a carbon copy of me. What worked in disciplining me as a child would not work with her.

I would have said "I love you" more.

I would have acknowledged that she processed information differently.

I would have stopped looking for the magic "fix," which may have given her the impression that she had more than a defective heart, that she was also a defective person.

UNSPEAKABLE!

February 17, 2005

Dear Courtney,

There must be unfinished business! Will "this business" ever be finished? I keep coming back, over and over, to the things I did or didn't do with you, for you. Apparently, there was so much anger and disappointment. You were so different from what I envisioned my daughter would be. I felt at times as though you were very much like your Grandma Nina in that we never could connect. Expectations were out of whack, and we couldn't connect even when we wanted to.

I wanted you to go "further" than I did; to do better than me. Did either of us want that? I doubt it. I'm competitive. I don't think you wanted to compete or were afraid to. How complicated our life was together! I was always trying to figure it out, to find a path we could both be on and still be separate people. Would we have found it?

I was dealt a tough hand to play in raising you! I think I did really well in the beginning because I believed that through my will, you would survive and thrive. It became complicated as you grew and expressed your own will and personality. I was not wise enough to shift gears. I was afraid that if I did, you would not survive without my vigilance. I still feel guilty. I try not to focus on that too much, as it is not good for me. When I find myself going over and over the past, I have to write to help sort it out and get rid of it—at least for a while.

I only refer to you in the past tense. That is all I can talk about to others. I need to describe who you were, the funny things you said and did. This is my "hell," my punishment, if there is such a thing! I look with longing at other thirty-four-year-olds and wonder what you would be like and what you would be doing. I look at their five-year-olds and long for a chance to hold you both.

Love,

Mom

March 20, 2005

My sixtieth birthday has come and gone. What a birthday celebration of dinners, a "surprise" party, and Ireland! I'm going to list what I've done or accomplished in these sixty years and what I have learned:

- I often feel as though I now know less than ever!

- I've obtained my goals in my work through perseverance.

- I learned to play the piano, flute, viola, and guitar.

- I learned to speak in public in high school. It has come in handy for making presentations and speeches throughout my life.

- I acquired an awareness of others' pain when I began working in mental institutions.

- I've learned that all families were not like mine, i.e., predictable, loving, and stable.

- I'm aware that people are carrying unimaginable burdens.

April 4, 2005

Yesterday I cried throughout most of the service that was on death. What I have learned and continue to learn: the numbness and the "silent witness" is always followed by a "meltdown." The tears started one by one and then increased—much to my dismay—and my attempts to hold them back failed. Our minister's description of the Indian tradition of cremation triggered memories of Courtney's ashes.

What I have learned is that these episodes, although not as frequent now, still come to the surface with an unexpected trigger to be dealt with yet again. I'm left with dismay and exhaustion. Again I am made aware that "It" is never over. There is never acceptance, although you tell yourself there is. There is never a bottom, no end to the grieving for a child lost.

(These feelings of despair disappear almost like magic after writing them down. I seem to be able to refocus, exercise, etc., and enjoy my family and friends—until the next time, of course.)

April 5, 2010

Spring!

Spring is bursting at the seams!

Birds are singing nonstop and making nests!

Camellias, forsythia are glorious!

Tulips, daffodils, and hyacinths are singing the praises of spring!

Another winter survived.

Another winter enjoyed.

Buried in snow,

No sight of a living thing except us.

This spring is special:

Rebirth has come yet again, singing its message over and over,

A cycle of birth and death.

Life goes on.

April 29, 2005

Upon the Birth of Our Great Nephew, Elijah Michael

What a miracle!

A new life!

A new beginning!

The cycle of life has begun again!

You have brought joy and hope!

You have brought laughter and awe!

UNSPEAKABLE!

You have given your grandparents a twinkle in their eyes!

You represent continuity!

You represent all that is good!

Where there has been grief, you have brought renewal and hope.

Elijah Michael Baker, welcome!

May 9, 2005

Mother's Day. We drove over to Winchester to spend it with Jason. It was a glorious day driving through the Virginia hill country.

We had a tasty brunch at an Old English restaurant. Afterward we went to a concert performed by developmentally disabled musicians whom Jason accompanied on drums.

The music was as though it had been picked just for us, the soundtrack of our lives:

"Sunrise, Sunset" from *Fiddler on the Roof*. John got up and left. It was too much.

Can we ever escape?!

June 28, 2005

What we have to be thankful for at this point in time:

- Our son

- Memories of Courtney

- Our cat Luna

- Friends

- Travel

- Our house near a lake and our backyard

- Barbecues with friends

August 26, 2005

It has been five years since Courtney died.

To My Friends

You never forget it!

You never get over it!

You never get beyond it!

The grief for a child continues, never ending.

UNSPEAKABLE!

I wish there were words to convey this to others,

understand my experience.

Do I really want them to experience this?

Alas! No words adequately describe the despair

nor the depth of my loss.

My recourse is to encourage my friends

to see my sorrow:

Give me a pat, a hug, a kiss on the cheek;

Listen to what I say with unconditional love and acceptance,

without an attempt to make me feel better;

Please accept that I will never be the same person

you used to know.

This is my spiritual path.

I see the world now with different eyes.

I hear with different ears.

My heart is

patched, and stitched to keep on beating.

Nevertheless it is broken.

CHAPTER 4

When Does the Pain Stop?

September 12, 2005

Dear Courtney,

I miss you! Nothing has changed in our acceptance of your death. In fact, your absence is as much felt by your dad and me as when you died five years ago! Your brother is in transition at best. Jason and Susan are getting a divorce. He tells us it's not about us and to forget her! She brought light and hope back into our lives after you died. She made your loss almost bearable. There was laughter in this house! Now nothing. None of the clichés work. We know that things don't turn out for the best. We don't know that things will get better. We're coping as best we can. Your dad is going to buy another boat. It gives him something to look forward to.

I am very angry and depressed right now. I didn't sign up for this. I didn't know what I was getting into! I guess no parent does. I'm being my "only child self," as you always put it. I don't like this game. I want to take my marbles and go home.

In the midst of all of this ruminating, Brian called. He seems to be doing fine. He has a new love interest. (Brian and his second wife divorced in 2004.) She's a KU grad! She's got to be great! They are planning on marrying before he goes back to Iraq. This time I feel much better about a new marriage for him. It's as it should be, don't you think? "They" say that when a man marries soon after his wife dies, it means that he had a good marriage and wants to find that again. We're looking forward to meeting her. He always says something funny, and I don't get into "shoulds" with him as I do with your brother. Brian's call ended the day on a positive note.

I didn't want you to be an "only child." Now I have one anyway. Is this a horrible joke? Is this path we're on our life lesson? I haven't a clue!

Love,

Your Mom

Later...

A mother's bond with her child is present in all mammals. A program on PBS tonight included humans, elephants, monkeys, and bears. In humans, it never goes away. It remains forever, even after death. Oh, the anguish I live with! It becomes commonplace.

One day I hope we will be so giddy with anticipation that we won't know what to do with ourselves! How long must we wait? How long does this lesson last? How long will we observe life from the outside looking in? Give us a hint so we can know that this torment won't last forever.

October 29, 2005

This is the "Day of the Dead" service at church. Should I speak? Do I have anything else to say? Am I flaunting my grief? Am I walking around with a "hair shirt" and want everyone to know how much I suffer? If I do share, this is what I will say:

I light this candle in remembrance of the children in our congregation who have passed.

I light this candle for John, myself, and all the other parents who have lost children.

December 27, 2005

Forty Years

The ups and downs, the highs and lows,

the adventures and the misadventures!

Our two precious children.

Our delight.

Our terror.

Our admiration.

Our support.

Our extended family and friends.

UNSPEAKABLE!

Our sunrises in China, Greece, and Costa Rica.

Our sunsets in Hawaii, California, England,

and on the Chesapeake.

Our laughter—at ourselves mostly.

Our tears, with no bottom yet found.

Our differences.

Our similarities.

Last but not least: our Love for each other.

January 2, 2006

A Prayer for the New Year

May we have Peace this New Year.

May our health continue to be good.

May our careers continue to serve the greater good,

as well as funding our lives.

May we contribute some of our prosperity to others.

May we continue to heal.

May we also help others to heal.

May we look for the "silver lining and seek the positive."

Blessings to our family and extended family in this New Year.

May 2006 be full of wonderful surprises!

March 30, 2006

Upon the Death of a Baby

Losing a child is unspeakable.

It is out of order.

It makes no sense.

You want to rewind the tape,

Rewrite the ending,

Find out the cause so you can correct this mistake.

Yet the reality is there.

She is gone as quickly as she arrived.

Will you be as before her entrance, her existence?

UNSPEAKABLE!

Sadly, no.

You are forever changed by this miracle come and gone.

Why did this happen?

What is the meaning, the lesson to be learned?

Perhaps you will at times have the irrational thought:

"Is this a punishment for some earlier transgression?"

All kinds of "crazy" thoughts and feelings and behaviors

are now new to you.

Sometimes, when you least expect it,

the loss will come flooding back.

There is a bond that cannot be broken.

That is what hurts.

The connection that can never cease.

You don't want it to cease.

April 29, 2006

You are Not Alone

Tears, memories, yearnings keep us connected.

Even the pleasant memories of a special day or moment

will give some ease.

You will go on.

There are other children to care for,

Other commitments to meet,

Other events to take pleasure in.

The years and milestones will go by.

You will learn to live without Them.

You won't stop yearning for Them,

Wondering what They would be like at any given age.

You are changed forever with the loss of this child.

No one knows except those of us with broken hearts.

UNSPEAKABLE!

June 27, 2006

Courtney and Brian's ninth anniversary. What a magical night! Perfect! I'm so happy she had the wedding she dreamed of.

June 28, 2006

A woman was interviewed on NPR who had lost her child. She had done research to find out whether there was a name for parents who have lost a child. What she found in her research: there is no name for us in any culture! I was astounded! I hadn't thought of that. When you lose your parents, she said, you are an "orphan." When you lose your spouse, you are a "widow." Widow comes from the Greek word "empty." We're empty, too, but that doesn't begin to describe us. No culture has been able to name parents who have lost children. It's too scary! It's unspeakable!

July 13, 2006

I need help! I need a vacation! I've become so negative and controlling. I feel the need to pick at both J's and tell them what to do. The negativity has also affected my work. I want life to go smoothly and always on an upward curve. When that doesn't happen, I'm angry. I'm angry, angry, *angry*! Angry that Jason has to pick up the pieces after his divorce. Angry that Courtney is gone. Angry when I listen to other people brag about the plans and accomplishments of their children. All I have is the past to talk about. I'm angry that I feel I'm imposing on my friends when I refer to Courtney. There's nothing for them to say...

I have to keep my mouth shut with Jason. He's reacting to every-thing. He needs to move out, and soon so he won't be under the microscope!. I'm angry that he's an only child now. No dilution of parental attention and expectations.

I need a vacation! All of my negative behaviors—selfishness, pee-vishness, negativity, etc.—are in full bloom. I have no patience. *I need a vacation!*

(I kept returning to the story and second-guessing myself.)

August 7, 2006

It's August

It's hot and muggy.

The leaves are still as green and lush as when you left us six years ago.

I have so many thoughts and feelings running around in my head.

This month brings our loss, our grief, our despair into focus.

Six years ago today I heard the baby's heartbeat.

I did not dare be elated.

I was scared!

UNSPEAKABLE!

Courtney, you are still with us!

We haven't forgotten you!

We cannot let go: it's impossible.

You are always with us—but most of all this month

when I remember your last days of life.

Neither your father nor I could do anything.

The trips to the ER, the migraines, the tachycardia.

You were coping with your own life.

You knew we were worried.

Indeed we were!

How different life would have been.

What kind of woman would you be now?

Would you still have health issues?

Perhaps another baby?

I imagine a grown woman in charge and involved in her family's life.

Her own person.

I'll never know.

WHEN DOES THE PAIN STOP?

There is no future now.

No hope.

Only this unrelenting despair.

Only "what-ifs,"

"Should haves."

The well of grief runs deep; it's bottomless!

*There are always fresh tears bubbling up from regions I can't
fathom.*

*I thought my sheer strength and determination would keep you
alive.*

And as I was trying to let go...this happened!

A mother is supposed to protect her child! I failed!

As unreasonable and negative as that sounds,

it's how I feel when I allow it.

In the depths of that well still remains

the guilt,

UNSPEAKABLE!

despair,

the failure

the punishment.

I was demanding,

Not listening,

Angry at you,

Disappointed in you.

I was the mother.

I should have been able to do this.

I could not.

I could not control events or you.

I failed.

I know you and I were formidable opponents at times,

"Cut from the same cloth," so to speak.

You are gone, and I have to live without a conclusion.

WHEN DOES THE PAIN STOP?

Open ended—

In fact, the way you preferred things to be.

The well of grief is endless when you lose a child.

Grief without end. Amen.

(I found the following letter from Courtney quite unexpectedly. There was no date, but it was probably around 1993.)

Mom,

I'm opening a new door in my life, and I find myself trying to find a way to close the old one. It's almost impossible to write this since I have never really acknowledged my feelings about this to you. This old door has to do with Pop's [grandfather] death. Since I have moved down to Florida, I've had to face a lot of memories, and you know I would much rather run from them than face them. Although Pop has never been far from my mind, I have avoided all attempts to bring him into a conversation because you would see how much pain it causes me to even think about him. I never wanted you to see it because I didn't think the way I was feeling was fair, especially to you. I have never said half of what I needed to say to you, and I definitely didn't with Pop. I just hope he knew he meant the world to me. So do you. Everything I have always done was always based on whether you would like it or not.

When Pop died, I built a wall between you and me and everyone I was supposed to love. I didn't think I could handle loving anyone after Pop. I find myself crying often, as I've done for the past six years. I don't have room to love or mourn anyone else. I know this is so wrong of me to have felt like this, but I have been so resentful towards you since he died, and for a while, I didn't understand it.

In some ways I held you responsible for his leaving me before I could tell him all I could and before I was old enough to know what needed to be said. I thought he died because you told him he would have to go into a rest home. I thought you didn't care how I felt because you never asked. Both of these feelings I know now are crap. I wasn't willing to talk to you or anyone about it. I preferred to be miserable.

Now I'm stuck with this pain, and I don't know where to put all the bad feelings and hope to keep the good. I think you are the only one who will understand. We finally need to talk about it. I want to remove the wall I built between us a long time ago and begin to rebuild the bond that was broken. Only you and me and a few others know how wonderful he was. I really believe he's an angel, or spiritual guide, somewhere doing more of what he did here.

I Love You So Much and Miss You,

Courtney

P.S. I'm sorry this letter took me so many years to write.

BLESSED BE!

August 31, 2006

Again the magnitude of our loss comes into full focus. It's almost as if the time in between the anniversary of her death, her birth, and wedding slips into a surreal place that protects us from the horror of it all - until It revisits us again.

Stuck

The last day of the worst month of the year.

The beginning of our seventh year without her.

The horror, the endless despair.

We are all very present with our loss.

No easing up.

No making peace with it.

How can we?

Courtney taught us so much.

Yes, we had her for twenty-eight and a half years instead of

Twenty-eight and a half days, hours, minutes.

It was not enough.

Yes, we have plenty of stories that make us laugh.

UNSPEAKABLE!

Her humor,

Her "do your own thing" philosophy,

Her creativity.

Still, her absence is a huge void underscored when we least expect it.

Are we stronger because we lost her?

Are we able to enjoy even the littlest things in life?

Are we only voyeurs of others' happiness?

I feel as though I'm waiting to exhale,

Waiting for life to be meaningful, exciting, motivating again.

I'm stuck.

October 19, 2006

Despair is back for the moment. I'm angry! I wake up at night. I talk to others about death and bereavement intellectually. Then spend two days crying off and on.

It delights me to see the little children in our lives grow and become real people. I cry for what has been taken away. The anger is so evident now. I react suddenly to unrelated issues or events. I assume I am going to get a negative reaction from others. Yet I get positive feedback from most.

I continue to focus on the negative. I worry about the future, John and Jason. This life seems like an endless ordeal, going from one crisis to another.

Haven't we experienced the worst? Yes. Still, we are in limbo. This flat, gray waiting to exhale is what it truly is. There are so many conflicting thoughts and feelings. I want to be close to those I love, yet I want to be separate and alone. I want to work until I'm sixty-five, yet I'm relieved when I'm not out there trying to make things happen. I want to continue to work, but I don't want the hassle or the stress that comes with it.

I am consciously trying not to control others. I get angry when I can't have my way. I want to be visible through volunteer work, but I also want to be isolated, insulated, with no demands.

I was not prepared for the issues confronting me. Who is? My parents, of course, had no idea what I would be faced with. Their lives had been so predictable. Why think about this? It is sometimes so hard to keep on keeping on. I don't know the right things to do or say anymore. I feel as though I'm in a straightjacket at times. How am I going to live out the rest of my life? We can't travel all the time as a temporary escape from the magnitude of our loss. How will I fill my days? "Be present" came to me during yoga. I'm writing it in my daily planner each day—if I remember!

We can never be what we were before losing Courtney. Maybe that goes without saying. The loss of a child with *her* child can't be accepted, can't be OK. Is all this confusion, anger, withdrawal, and paranoia a reaction to my loss of Courtney and her baby? Probably. Six years after her death, there are layers upon layers of this experience with no end—perhaps resting places, but they don't last long.

November 18, 2006

I Haven't Accepted Death

I cry when animals in the wild are killed.

I cry for the father who found the body of his daughter in the woods.

I cry for the soldier killed in Iraq.

Death is real to me.

It plays no favorites.

It takes at random.

It takes us all eventually, doesn't it?

I knew this.

I was taught this.

It was the "old ones."

How still they were,

Their hands hard and unmoving in the casket.

I wasn't prepared to lose a child.

Of course children died, but not mine.

WHEN DOES THE PAIN STOP?

Children died in the "camps" in the '40s.

Grandparents of natural causes in the '50s

In the '60s, death came close to home:

A president assassinated.

A close friend's helicopter down in Vietnam, dead at twenty-six!

Families forever grieving.

I haven't accepted death as a part of life, not when it's my child.

I can pontificate and make it sound as though I have it worked out.

On a gut level, it's a different story.

I feel the despair of others and their feelings of hopelessness.

All the trite phrases come to mind.

Who said it was going be a "rose garden"?

"Why do bad things happen to good people?"

The bottom line: I haven't accepted death!

Why us?

UNSPEAKABLE!

Why Courtney?

Why the suffering?

No, I haven't accepted death.

I rail against it!

I shake my fist at it!

I expend energy that should be used productively somewhere else!

January 1, 2007

Affirmations for 2007

May I be happy.

May I be healthy.

May my love for John and Jason continue to grow and give me solace.

May my work continue to challenge me and expand.

May I treat all people with consideration and sensitivity.

May I be fearless.

May I confront obstacles.

WHEN DOES THE PAIN STOP?

May I see the glass half full.

May I accept how my life has unfolded.

May I be there for my friends.

May I see life and events as not always about me.

May I truly believe that I can accomplish anything,

Believe that I can accept and cope with anything that life has to offer.

May I be present and not in the past or the future but in the now.

May I control what I reasonably can and let go of things I can't.

May I have a truly fantastic year in every way!

March 11, 2007

Sixty-two years! Another marker. Another milestone. A milestone on a journey.

Recently my friend of forty-eight years and I reminisced about how we used to look forward to our sixteenth, seventeenth, and eighteenth birthdays! Today it's another day, another year. There is no longer the heady anticipation of getting our driver's licenses, graduation, and a beer. It's the hope for health, our children's happiness, maybe an exciting trip.

Most people don't believe I'm sixty-two! It used to be effortless to stay in shape. Today it's a conscious mindfulness of the benefits of yoga, exercise, meditation, and diet to have the energy and perseverance to cope with what life dishes out. What have I learned this past year? How many steps have I taken toward nirvana?

Grief has eased for now, though the pain is always there in the background. Sharing parts of my journal has been healing. I need to publish it for other parents who have lost children. It may be of help to someone.

I need to mind my own business professionally and personally. My need to control and not put in my two cents' worth remain an issue. Also keeping my mouth shut and knowing when to open it is another issue. I blame my genes, specifically my mother and grandmother's! It's no excuse!

What is the greatest desire of my heart this sixty-second year?

- To see Courtney! To feel her presence!

- To see John appreciated and enjoying his work.

- Jason and Brian happy and fulfilled.

- To be healthy and active, yet still have time to be quiet.

- To have Brian and all soldiers come home.

- To have peace!

June 1, 2007

I woke up! My mind is going around and around. I visit anxiety, then on to worry, panic, and grief. I'm definitely not the person I used to be, yet people see me as strong. I wonder what they see? It must be the mask I put on everyday. I see my life filtered through this screen of grief, of PTSD, and the candle I light everyday before yoga and meditation. I continue to have questions: Can I continue to sell real estate? What do I want to do with the rest of my life? Why does everything feel like a mountain to climb?

June 6, 2007

The "worm has turned" and I'm on top of my game. I'm getting things done. I'm sleeping better. I'm enjoying the quiet as well as the busyness. The questions are still the same, but there is also a calm acceptance of their presence.

August 22, 2007

A friend died on August 5 in a motorcycle accident. What is it about August? Next Monday, it will be seven years. Our lives are circumscribed by the anniversary. I still miss her and her baby. At times like this I feel no hope.

August 24, 2007

Today we're placing flowers on Courtney's grave for the umpteenth time. Jason will be with us today. The cemetery is such an empty place. I feel empty and resigned when I'm there, as if I am done with it. I know full well I'm not. We need to go there. It pays tribute to her life. We'll be going out to get something to eat afterward. In some way it comforts us to nourish our bodies—to be in the present, not the past.

August 30, 2007

Time

It still feels like 2000.

We're zombies.

Life washing over us.

Trying to get through the day.

Where has time gone?

Time stands still for us.

We eat.

We breathe.

We laugh.

We cry and cry and cry.

Time goes on, and still it's August 2000.

October 8, 2007

I finally joined one of the groups in our church whose members choose a topic and then share thoughts and feelings about it. Tonight was our first meeting: two men and the rest women. Our assignment was to bring a photograph of something special in our lives. I brought the Ansel Adams photo of the Grand Tetons. Everyone else, except the two men, brought family pictures. There was a lot of sharing about mothers, daughters, grandchildren, and stepchildren, etc.

I feel as though I'm an alien! However, I think it will be good for me to sit and listen and not try to be the center of attention, like I usually do. I'll get to know people on a whole different level. Tonight I was overwhelmed by the absence of Courtney. It underscored how empty and fractured my life is. I really don't know whether I can do this or not.

November 19, 2007

John had his second cataract operation today. While I was sitting in the waiting room reading, I noticed a large woman with her three equally large daughters. Soon after, I saw other mothers with their daughters. I began to look for similar characteristics. I wondered what Courtney would look like now and if people would still recognize us as mother and daughter. Immediately, the feeling of loss began to "bubble up" with the shock and horror that she is gone. The tears came to my eyes. I buried myself in my book. A few years ago, I would have left the room to recover someplace else. Today I was the "silent witness," observing mothers with their daughters.

UNSPEAKABLE!

December 13, 2007

Tuesday I went to our company Christmas party at the Elkridge Furnace Inn where Courtney and Brian were married in 1997. Big mistake! I was OK until I walked past the main staircase where Courtney and Brian had their final picture at their wedding reception. The company luncheon took place in the same tent where their reception took place. A further mistake was using the restroom on the third floor, where Courtney and her bridesmaids got dressed! Tears could not be held back for long. What a happy day for Courtney and Brian! What a magical day for all of us! They had so much hope for the future. Courtney, Brian, and I had so much fun planning the day. We pulled it off without one fight. What a miracle!

John and I have received an invitation to another wedding at the Elkridge Furnace Inn. I had been there several times simply to stand where Courtney's wedding had taken place overlooking the Patapsco River. I never went inside until our company party. It was an unexpected impact. I told him we needed to have dinner there a couple of times to desensitize him before the wedding.

Grief truly never ends. It continues intermittently forever: drop by drop, tear by tear, into a bottomless pool of endless longing for a life cut short.

December 29, 2007

Waiting

We still wait.

Sometimes I hear voices outside.

WHEN DOES THE PAIN STOP?

Is that you coming in, slamming the door? Calling "Mom"?

Your energy was evident the minute

you entered the house full of stories,

complaints,

life!

We still hang your stocking every Christmas.

We wait.

We wait for the pain to go away.

We wait for young faces to focus on.

We wait while we rush around making preparations

to fill this house again.

There is no filling it up.

No smell of roast beef and carrot pudding brings you back

or lessens the void.

Nothing eases the loss of you.

Nothing takes the place of you!

January 9, 2008

I've made an intention for this year: to be present, not to worry too much, and not to dwell on the past. Every night before I go to sleep, I will write down all the things for which I'm grateful.

(Note that there is no entry on Courtney's birthday, January 21. I'm sure we marked the day by a cemetery visit and her favorite dinner. I found that when I didn't have the compulsion to write every day, I told myself that I was making progress and things were getting better.)

January 27, 2008

It's the twenty-seventh. That number reminds me of joy and sorrow: our wedding, Courtney and Brian's wedding, her death.

Today I got to church early to rehearse for the morning's services. I had no problem during rehearsal singing one of the hymns. However, when we sang the same hymn during the service, the tears started. We sang something about watching a child grow. The second verse was about death. More tears rolling down my cheeks. This time I couldn't suck it up and go on. I had to go home. John and I walked around Centennial Lake later that day.

(The following poem began to form as we walked. As soon as I got home, I was compelled to write it down, as it reflected my feelings at the time.)

The Well

Grief is like a deep well.

A well with no bottom, no end.

A well of limitless sadness.

An abyss where, from time to time, one falls and falls and falls.

No end to tears.

No end to cries of despair.

No end to pain.

Only echoes of what was.

Only "shadows on the wall of a cave."

I've kept a light burning in her window this season of hope,

This month of her birth.

Still waiting for a sign, as if she will magically appear.

Magical thinking never stops,

Never ends.

Maybe if I'm quiet enough,

UNSPEAKABLE!

Kind enough,

Meditate enough;

Maybe if I do enough penance,

Enough good deeds;

Maybe I'll see her, feel her touch, hear her voice again.

March 11, 2008

Sixty-three! Boy, am I getting old! There was a rainbow the other day, which always reminds me of Courtney. I shake my head and realize life continues to go on. I used to think as time passed, after the death of a loved one, the easier it becomes. I don't think *easier* is the right word. The minute I say something like that the opposite occurs soon after. Overall, losing Courtney isn't as raw as it used to be, and I'm amazed at the fun I can have.

My longtime friend spent a week with us. Every time we get together, we laugh ourselves silly over all the funny things that happened during those grade school through high school years. Laughing is so important; I've been told that it releases a chemical that lifts your spirits and promotes a feeling of well being. I love to laugh, and I need to do more of it!

March 31, 2008

What a month! Business is picking up client-wise and location-wise.

Our office at Re/Max has moved into a bigger space. So far we all like the change. Speaking of change, John is retiring from the government. How did this happen? It seems as though he just got his first job! I've planned a party. His brother and nephew are flying in from Wisconsin to surprise him. I hope this comes together without John finding out. We're planning on toasting him and wishing him an exciting future filled with good health, travel, sailing, skiing, and softball!

June 29, 2008

It's the summer solstice, with its long days and warm weather. Rain, too.

It's been eleven years since Courtney and Brian's wedding. I'm glad she and Brian were married in 1997. After all, it was on her "bucket list."

Friends from out of town were here last weekend for a sail. Their first grandchild is on the way. They have lots to look forward to. I had a meltdown after they left. I felt sick—didn't want to move. This season was Courtney's last. The summer teaming with life. It brings it all back into focus. John had a meltdown, too, while watching a movie last night.

The following week was a surprise! We received a call from a member of our extended family asking us to be "honorary" grandparents. The christening is to be September 6. Her brother's engagement party will be at that time, too.

We also received free tickets to hear a string quartet with dinner afterwards. On Friday, we'll hear a friend's band play outdoors at Clyde's.

UNSPEAKABLE!

I'm laughing at everything to the annoyance of John. Either I've become manic or I've been given a break, or both!

What else does the summer hold? Sailing with friends, our niece and her husband coming for a visit, and my forty-fifth high school reunion!

September 17, 2008

Good Morning!

Yoga last night was so good. The theme for the class was about stages we go through in life: spirit, birth, family, career, retirement, returning once again to spirit. That concept will be something to think about this coming week.

Guilt was coming up before yoga, guilt about how I was as a mother. Courtney and I somehow got off track. My sister-in-law is so patient and positive with her family and students. That is what loved ones need, not someone who challenges and criticizes. I was so panicked over Courtney's underachieving in school that I couldn't see the forest for the trees. Jason recently told us that during all the angst with Courtney, he preferred to be "under the radar" rather than adding more problems for us to deal with. I must quit blaming myself for the choices Courtney made in her teens. There-in lies my regret: I'll never have the chance to relax, praise, and encourage her.

September 19, 2008

The following is a writing assignment as part of the class, "The Artist's Way." This was a significant event and one that I want to preserve.

A good friend had a gathering of women at her house tonight. I knew that Robin, a psychic, was going to be there to do readings for twenty minutes each. I thought it would be the usual parlor game full of generalities, etc. When it was my turn, I sat down in a wingback chair. Robin took several deep breaths and then asked me to say my full name three times. I slowly said "Kay Armstrong Baker". Immediately she began to cry. She said there was a deep sense of sadness surrounding me. More tears. Then she said my daughter was near. Robin asked my permission to "invite" Courtney in. Throughout this time, Robin continued to cry. I couldn't believe what I was seeing! Courtney, through Robin, said that she loved me. She also said that she wanted me to write letters to her. She was at peace and happy. Courtney said she was progressing towards becoming a "spiritual guide." Apparently, she was quite proud of her progression to the next level. While this was being said, Robin moved in a way that was so like Courtney when she was pleased with herself. At that point Robin said she saw Courtney hugging me. I said, through my tears, I was glad she was happy, but we weren't. We missed her!

Our time was up.

The other women had the mundane, "parlor game", readings that I expected. I don't know what to think. John certainly doesn't believe in that stuff, but when I told him, he was polite and listened.

UNSPEAKABLE!

January 3, 2009

John and I saw the movie, *Frost/Nixon* with some friends. It was a great movie! The acting was good, in fact, excellent. I started to get upset when there was a scene taking place in June 1972.

I said to myself, *Courtney was alive during this time.* Another scene had an infant crying in the background. One tear, then two, then another. *Stop, refocus,* I said to myself. At the end of the movie, the emotion began "bubbling up" again. *Refocus!*

As we walked to a restaurant afterward, John asked me what had been the matter during the movie. I said I would tell him later. One tear, two tears, and a few more. *Refocus!* During dinner I told him I had become upset because Courtney was alive when this story took place. Refocus! Eat your dinner. Nourish yourself.

Finally after we got home, the dam broke. I just started to sob, saying, "She was alive!. The sobbing turned to wailing, then to keening. All the while John held me. It came from deep inside me. Almost like from a pit, a bottomless pit. It came from the core of my being: the despair, the hurt, the disappointment, the anger, the loss of a child and all a child means to a parent—the holidays, the empty chair at the table, Brian with his new wife. It just gets to be too much. So much to keep under wraps. So much energy expended on keeping it together. I write and write about "It". "It" never goes away. It's always there. Then, when you least expect "It", out of nowhere, with a tiny sentence or word, insignificant to anybody else, comes the outpouring of grief.

What an interesting and awful process to watch. Yes, I was watching what was happening to me during and after the movie, much as I do when I meditate. I was feeling the sound come from my soul. I was hearing the pitch start low and then go higher and higher.

Then it subsided almost as suddenly as it started. I felt released, relaxed, and very tired. I've only done that one other time: the day Brian and Jen came to pick up the china that he and Courtney had selected before their wedding.

Hopefully, whatever it was has been released until next time. I'll share this with my counselor. I still think I have many shards, like broken glass, sticking in me. Maybe one was released last night, but there are more there. There always will be.

January 21, 2009

I almost wrote 1972! It's Courtney's birthday. She would have been thirty-seven. It's been eight and a half years since her death. John has the worst case of the flu I've ever seen. I don't think he'll be going with me to the cemetery.

Barack Obama was sworn in as president yesterday. What a day to celebrate! Things have got to turn around for this country—he can't do it all! It's a very emotional day and time for just about everybody. How can it not be? It is truly a milestone, a paradigm shift. I heard Martin Luther King's speeches in the sixties. I saw the riots in 1967 on TV. I lived in the South where older blacks would not rock the boat for fear of reprisals. We saw the horrific news coverage: the protests in Alabama and Mississippi, the water hoses, the attack dogs, and the police with clubs.

Today Obama has the challenge of repairing our relations with Europe while at the same time getting the country back on its feet in housing, jobs, energy, and health care. There's new energy in the White House: the Obama girls doing normal things such as sleepovers. How can it not lift our spirits?

UNSPEAKABLE!

Courtney has missed so much, or has she? We miss her more and more, not less and less. I think after the shock of her death, the grief shifts over time to a dull ache—especially losing a child—and gets sharper at different times of the year. Although we enjoy seeing Brian (*we need to see him*), it's always difficult afterward. Seeing him emphasizes the fact that Courtney is gone.

I have my session with my counselor tomorrow. What will come up this time? I told my acupuncturist when I had my last treatment that it seemed as though I watched others go on with their lives. Our friends now have grandchildren. Some are expecting a grandchild for the first time. Not us. We wait and watch.

Jason's fiancée, Rebecca, has a birthday Friday. I have a present for her. It is a photograph taken in Egypt of a belly dancer and a man playing a drum. Rebecca is a belly dancer, and Jason is a drummer. I only saw the dancer when I bought it. Another so-called "coincidence."

It's the despair that still sits with me. If I was truly in the moment, I would acknowledge my grief and move on. I know I've written this before, but the grief goes round and round. Same feelings, only different years, different times. Courtney's sudden death changed us all. It's not like anger, which lasts a few minutes and then it is done. The death of a child settles into your whole being, and even though one refocuses and does what needs to be done" It" remains, quiet, waiting for expression yet again. I don't think professionals who haven't personally experienced the death of their own child really know what I'm talking about. How can they? We don't hang on to our grief because we like to feel bad. We don't hang on to "It" because we like the attention. "It" just is. "It" is part of who we are now.

Thirty-seven years ago was a paradigm shift for us, too. Courtney's birth was a transforming experience. I was higher than a kite at her birth, and totally present, with little medication. The high stayed with me throughout the next few days and weeks, while we slowly digested the fact that our baby had a serious heart defect. John and I have never been the same since.

CHAPTER 5

Going On

February 28, 2009

I Saw You

I saw you swinging in the park.

You appeared, unbidden,

Out of the blue.

You were swinging.

Your long red hair streaming behind you.

Swinging high.

Enjoying the balmy February day.

I sat in my car at the stop sign watching this vision.

So exuberant.

So free.

You turned and knew I saw you.

I took a breath,

Wiped the tears away,

And went on with my day.

March 12, 2009

Another birthday come and gone.

Sixty-four, yet again I wonder how I got here.

Wasn't it just yesterday that I was forty-six? Twenty-six? Sixteen?

Time. How to understand it, get my head around it.

Accept it!

Enjoy it!

Jason and Rebecca came over to fix me breakfast complete with Eggs Florentine, flowers, and blueberry juice. It was a wonderful way to start the day. Cards followed, along with e-mails, a movie, and dinner. I went off my Lenten fast of no sugar and alcohol. Today I'm paying for it!

UNSPEAKABLE!

May 11, 2009

Another Mother's Day. Only one chick left in the nest, so to speak. Jason and Rebecca fixed dinner for me last night. Lots of toasts to mothers. Brian called. He has been involved in more military training. He'll be back here in July. We'll get him out on the boat. Heather is done with her doctorate and will move to Colorado Springs in June. We teased him that now the real work starts. He said it's going to bring their marriage to a whole new level. John piped in, "Like honey-do lists!"

Another bittersweet day. I did some yard work and planted three tomato plants. I hope they produce tomatoes!

June 9, 2009

Lots of "stuff" bubbling up again. I saw a foreign film about a woman who had spent fifteen years in prison for killing her six year old son. The major theme was her re-entry into society and the various rejections and problems within her family when she was released from prison. Toward the end of the movie, her sister finds a document of the boy's diagnosis. His condition was terminal, and the boy was in a lot of pain. The mother euthanized him. The last scene was the mother screaming and crying to her sister about it. The lines that I remember were "You give birth to a child only to watch him die." And another: "When you lose a child, it is like being in an eternal prison." Basically, her years in prison made no difference to her as she already saw herself imprisoned.

I could certainly identify with the movie. It goes down to my very core: the "silent scream," the void we all live with. Jason says he can sense when one of his teenagers at work has had a loss. He doesn't always know what it is, but he knows the kid is grieving.

Last fall I wrote over and over about my anger. Now I feel as though I've said what I needed to say, and it is done.

June 28, 2009

We're on the boat for a very relaxing weekend. We had perfect wind conditions all the way to Wharton Creek. All on the same tack! We got up here Friday and just vegged all day yesterday. We were ready for the rest of the sailing club to join us and raft up.

Today it's early. Clear pinkish/orange clouds as the sun is coming up. Where we dropped anchor, we saw the sunset last night. It was glorious! The bald eagle we saw last year has shown himself again.

It's so quiet now. No one is up, only the birds and me.

It was twelve years ago Courtney and Brian got married. Twelve years! It never seems possible. Just a distant memory now, a longing—not the bite as in previous years. As I write this, with the boat gently rocking, I feel cared for, supported, and loved. The intense feelings may come back to bite me yet again. Right now, I'm totally in the moment.

July 7, 2009

It's been almost nine years since Courtney died. How have we lived this long with the pain of her absence? The pain, agony, and yes, the pleasures we enjoy: our cat, Mr. Luna. He is so swift! He loves to run across the backyard. He loves his life with us, and we love him. Whatever the true essence of cats is, they are magical, spiritual beings. I never thought about animals, cats or dogs, as anything other than what they were on the surface. However, as I've gotten older, I sense a whole different presence within them. I'm talking about Garfield, Max, and Luna in particular. However, since Courtney died, I do feel I connect with the spirit of everything. I don't know why exactly, but I feel the life force now—even with plants!

August 6, 2009

The pall of August is upon us. Every year I write the same thing. Nine years! Courtney's death still doesn't seem real. It gradually sets in little by little: the lack of enthusiasm. Who knows how It manifests Itself in me and to others? Possibly no one remembers or notices. It's almost like a ball and chain that impedes everything. In spite of that, we've been sailing more—two days at a time, which is not enough to relax and renew. I've been reading a lot and making lots of gazpacho! It's an escape.

This month we are having an engagement party for Jason and Rebecca. It is the week of the anniversary of Courtney's death. A few years ago, that would have been out of the question, and yet we said, "Yes, we'll do it." Life somehow goes on.

We've seen Brian, too, which is good. He always makes time for us.

It's raining a slow rain. August is so difficult now, almost the end of summer and the long, lush, sultry days. This is what she saw her last days. Courtney was in her prime and full of life. The Sunday before she died, she picked crabs with John and me and talked about her plans for the baby and her life as an Army wife. Today I remember the crows cawing in the trees day after day. Some native people believe the crow is a harbinger of death. The chair she sat in broke that week. One of the two oak trees that stood together was cut down. Many trips to the hospital. She was a twenty-eight-year-old coping with health issues in a seventy-eight-year-old body. This is what August is to us. Year after year. A little less pain but pain nonetheless and an emptiness, an ache in our hearts for our lost cub.

August 16, 2009

The pall continues though we, on the surface, make the best of it. We just got back from an overnight on the boat. It was hot and humid but still pleasant, ending in a picnic with the club. I've caught a cold, I suspect, from sitting in the petri dish of the Patient First clinic with a piece of glass in my foot. In addition I pulled a muscle in my back while pulling on lines. My body is reacting to this month, too.

The sting, the horror, the disbelief has receded from nine years ago. It pops up, and I acknowledge it, but in less frequent moments. It's intense when it happens but then subsides. We all miss Courtney immensely. She is a part of our past, which I'm tending to examine and think about more and more.

The engagement party is next Sunday. I didn't realize that it was so close to the anniversary of Courtney's death. *(I apparently had no recollection that I had just written this a few days before. The "blocking," the "forgetting" remains.)* This year I'm hoping it will be a distraction and not a ball and chain. I always rise to the occasion somehow.

August 23, 2009

(Again and again the week of her death, we relive that day whether we want to or not.)

Reprise

Snow falling in Kansas the day she was born,

Silent, soft,

Awestruck by its beauty.

A sunny Sunday morning the day she died.

Bagels outside, greeting the day

Masking the horror yet to come.

Thunder, lightning the day she died.

Visibility almost nonexistent.

We had to get home!

To safety?

To life as it was that morning?

Shock! Disbelief!

Our hearts ripped apart,

Forever broken.

With time it won't hurt so much they say.

As quickly as I write this

I am pulled back to that day of horror,

That day of the "Unspeakable."

Instantly she is in focus,

Her absence palpable,

The void felt.

The void within us.

Today her spirit will be with us.

Today—quiet, warm, expectant.

Today we are looking forward, not backward.

UNSPEAKABLE!

Today we happily prepare for a celebration, not a memorial service.

How odd!

An engagement party!

We joyfully welcome our new family!

Today we are hopeful for a new future for Jason, for us.

Today we focus on him and Rebecca.

Today is her brother's day.

Jason and Rebecca's day!

Today we celebrate!

Courtney as a Big Sister

I was an only child and knew nothing of the day-to-day relationship between siblings. I took a dim view at times of the bickering, fighting, and competition that is normal (so I'm told) between brothers and sisters. I had grown up in a quiet household, unless of course I chose to turn up the volume. In looking back on their relationship, I like to remember Courtney as the loving and responsible Big Sister.

Courtney was three years and four months old at the time Jason was born. Courtney and I talked a lot about the baby to come. I bought her the book , Betsy's Baby Brother by Gunilla Wolde. We would talk about how Betsy helped her mother take care of the new baby, such as entertaining him, giving her mother the baby powder, etc. Another book was, A Child Is Born: The Drama of Life Before Birth by A. Ingelman-Sundberg. Courtney was fascinated by the pictures of a baby in various stages of development in Mommy's tummy. We would talk frequently about his development as the pregnancy progressed month to month. She would put her hand on my stomach to feel the baby move. I talked about how the baby would not be able to do much at first. He would have to be fed, diapered, and bathed. But she would still be able to hold him and push him in the stroller. He would like that. I thought I had Courtney fully prepared to receive this new addition to the family.

When the day finally came, May 19, 1975, Jason Armstrong Baker was born. I had a C-section due to the umbilical cord presenting first. The baby was a ten on the Apgar Scale! Jason's birth added another dimension to Courtney's life. I called her as soon as I could get my wits about me to tell her she indeed had a baby brother. The first thing she asked was, "Does he have a penis?" We have her on film rushing to the door to see him when we brought him home. After a few days, Courtney pronounced Jason "boring"!

It didn't take long before she helped take charge of this happy, roly-poly baby. As Jason grew, Courtney would indeed entertain him. It wasn't all positive for her; her self-confidence slipped a little. Naturally some of the time she wanted all of my attention, as in the days prior to his birth.

Courtney was like a nanny to Jason. I remember telling others that Courtney was so responsible that if they got lost, she would figure out what to do. That is a bit of an exaggeration, but it pointed out her approach to taking care of her little brother.

This was best illustrated when I took the train to New York City with a seven-year-old and a three-year-old to visit friends and their children. I wanted to visit New York City before we moved to California. John was already there in his new job, while we waited for the house to be sold. In looking back on this trip, I can't believe I did it! It was January, so I had to take a lot of clothes, boots, jackets, etc. I managed to get all of it into one large suitcase. We took the train, which was a new experience for both of them. As we were pulling into Penn Station, I realized my folly. With no offer of assistance with my luggage (after all, this wasn't Minneapolis!), we got off the train. I told Courtney, sensing my vulnerability alone with two children, to take Jason's hand and stay close to me. I remember adding, "When I say jump, you say how high, and do what I say!" My concern was warranted; there were men loitering, leaning against the columns of the station, and watching us as we made our way to the Long Island Railroad. All this time Courtney took charge of Jason, and we made it to our destination!

A couple months later, in March 1979, we moved to California. At that time, Courtney would see the cardiologist once a year. She was an excellent role model for Jason, as she did not cry or fuss at the doctor's office even when she got an EKG or a shot.

Courtney wanted to join the local swim team and play soccer, which were both available to first graders. I was concerned about her participating in rigorous activities; however, the cardiologist thought it would be good for her—and us, too. He didn't want us to treat Courtney as an invalid and overprotect her, as some parents with children with heart defects tended to do.

The swim coach expected the swimmers to be at the pool early in the morning. Courtney got up and got to the pool, in the fog and chill of the California morning, and practiced her strokes and relays without complaint. Of course she was blue with cold afterward and in need of a snack. One year she received the award for "Most Improved". I took a picture of Courtney proudly holding her trophy, with Jason sitting next to her with a frown on his face. He had wanted to get an award like his sister! After that, there developed a competition between the two. Even so, Courtney would play Legos with Jason, and it was their best activity together.

Most of the time, Courtney ruled the roost, so to speak. Her powers of persuasion with Jason knew no bounds—from cats to ant farms to scary movies. She brought her little brother right along with her. In those grade school days, Courtney and Jason looked quite a bit alike. Some folks thought they were twins, especially when they were in the pool. One day she persuaded him to put on one of her dresses and a wig and made him up to look like a girl! Courtney took him to a neighbor's house and introduced him as her cousin. How nice of Courtney to bring her cousin over to meet her. She soon realized that it was Jason!

Jason, to his credit, had a sense of humor and liked to tease her. He liked to fiddle with radios or anything that had a knob or button. One day he "accidentally" set her alarm clock with the volume turned up. It went off in the middle of the night. Of course she woke up, out of a deep sleep, screaming. Jason, to this day, says he didn't do it on purpose!

Courtney and Jason were visiting their grandparents in Florida one summer. Jason caught a chameleon early in the morning and decided to have some fun with it. He caught the lizard and tiptoed back into the house. The neighbors across the street saw this and were waiting to hear the reaction. Jason dangled it over Courtney and told her to wake up. Her screams were heard all over the neighborhood!

UNSPEAKABLE!

Courtney, unfortunately, had a tendency to lie when it served her purposes especially if it got her brother in trouble. We had just moved back to Maryland from California. Uprooting kids aged fourteen and eleven is not easy, and there was a lot of angst and fighting between them. We were renting a townhouse until we could settle on our house and move in. A few days before Halloween, they got into a fight. I was scolding Courtney about fighting with her brother. Courtney was saying that he started it and was threatening her. All of a sudden, Jason blew up and threw a table knife into the kitchen wall!

Now, at thirty-seven, Jason tells me that Courtney lied and knew that he did not intend to stab her. Since my back was turned, all I saw was the knife sticking in the wall. I was stunned! I knew Jason was angry, but I believed Courtney. Regardless of what happened, it was grossly unacceptable. Jason was grounded and could not participate in any Halloween activities—much to Courtney's satisfaction, I'm sure!

At the time of her death, the two were beginning to relate to each other as adults.

October 30, 2009

It's Halloween again, Courtney's time. Courtney's favorite holiday. Every year since her death, I hope, I wait, I look for some sign from her now that the veil is thin between the two worlds. Maybe it will be this year. I know, intellectually, that this is magical thinking, but I don't care. Maybe I'll have a dream—a lucid dream like John has. Maybe...

A friend at work said she dreamed of me the other night with a pair of red-headed twin boys. It made me feel warm with anticipation, especially in light of the wedding in a few days. I made the mistake of telling John. I think he's afraid to hope that we could be blessed in such a way.

November 6, 2009

We're in Sedona preparing for Jason and Rebecca's wedding. We're staying at the Briar Patch Inn overlooking Oak Creek Canyon. No phone or TV. What a relief! Brian and Heather arrive tomorrow.

I had a flashback Wednesday while getting my nails done. A little girl was having her hair cut. Afterward her grandmother painted her nails. It reminded me of when I painted Courtney's nails when she was little. It starts as a slow drip, but it just keeps on until "It" expresses the full magnitude of my loss. Hopefully I've tapped and emptied the vessel of grief so I'll be able to get through the next few days.

The sermon by our minister, Rev. Paige Getty, this past Sunday was a challenge in as much as it was a series of poems by a mother whose daughter had been murdered. The book from which she read was called *Slamming Open the Door* by Kathleen Sheeder Bonanno. My minister had sent me an e-mail informing me of the service, so I would be prepared. The poems were tough to hear. I had to hold myself together to get through it. I managed somehow to place a stone in the water (during the "Stones of Joys and Sorrows" portion of our service) for the upcoming wedding in our family, as well as another stone for all the parents who have lost children. It's still unspeakable!

January 12, 2011

I woke up late to find a winter wonderland outside. After I write a little, I'm going for a walk to enjoy the air and the delightful snow. Sunday, I had planned on going to church. John and I were at the breakfast table and the TV was on. A commercial came on showing a very old couple intending to visit their children and their twin grandchildren. Instead the parents handed over the twins and left! The grandfather with one of the babies shuffles after them, saying, "Don't leave us with the babies! Don't leave us with the babies!" We laughed and said that if we were ever grandparents, we'd probably be that old! John said the commercial reminded him of when my parents took care of Courtney and Jason when we went to China. They were nine and six at the time. Why I went further with the memory, I don't know. *(One day my parents told Courtney she couldn't do something. She got mad at them. She was crying and saying, "I want my mother! You can't tell me what to do!")* At that point in recalling the memory, I started to cry, remembering what she said. "I want my mother." I couldn't stop crying and was a mess the rest of the day. Obviously I didn't go to church. I finally perked up when I watched a Kansas basketball game!

I miss her! When I see young adults her age, I wonder what Courtney would be like today. Would she have had only one child, our little grandson? Would she and Brian have worked on their marriage with all the stress that goes with being in the Army right now? I would like to think that our relationship would have continued to improve as she got older and we distanced ourselves from her volatile adolescence and early twenties. I'll never know.

January 4, 2012

I will continue my journal as I've developed a need to write almost everyday. Can I now "let go" and "move on"? I can't answer that question. I have found myself writing over and over again about my despair, anger and hope during the past eleven years since Courtney's death. It is my wish that you have been consoled, given hope and were able to identify with some of my feelings and experiences shared here.

I end this with a poem that was read at Courtney's memorial service:

Ascension
by Colleen Hitchcock

And if I go,

while you're still here...

Know that I live on,

vibrating to a different measure

—behind a thin veil you cannot see through.

You will not see me,

so you must have faith.

I wait for the time when we can soar together again,

—both aware of each other.

Until then, live your life to its fullest.

191

UNSPEAKABLE!

And when you need me,

Just whisper my name in your heart,

...I will be there.

CPSIA information can be obtained at www.ICGtesting.com
Printed in the USA
BVOW05s2110160314

347720BV00010B/174/P